ENDORSEMENTS

> *Mended* is a must-read! It is a transparent narrative of a couple who lacked basic communication skills that nearly destroyed a marriage and family. This real-life story of brokenness and redemption can help safeguard existing and future marriages from unnecessary trauma. It offers hope for couples who feel like there is no solution to their troubled marriage.
>
> **JOSH McDOWELL**
> AUTHOR AND SPEAKER

> Get ready for an incredible story of redemption. Rick and Tiffany's real-life account of a gut-wrenching affair and eventual restoration of their marriage is breathtaking. Read *Mended*—you'll not only be inspired by their story of reconciliation, but will learn how to affair-proof your own relationship. Every couple who wants to strengthen their marriage will benefit from this compelling book.
>
> **DRS. LES AND LESLIE PARROTT**
> #1 NEW YORK TIMES BESTSELLING AUTHORS OF *SAVING YOUR MARRIAGE BEFORE IT STARTS*

> What shouts boldly from the pages of *Mended* is the ultimate and powerful work of Christ! As 2 Corinthians 5:18 states, 'All this is from God, who reconciled us to himself through Christ and gave us the ministry of reconciliation.' This insightful, in-depth work of the Bulman family's miraculous restoration doesn't skirt any issues but boldly speaks the truth about the destructiveness of sin and its resulting pain. In the face of the factual, the entrance of God's redemption is on display. I applaud the courageous stance taken by this Kingdom couple to tell their story so that many may be safeguarded or saved from hell's strategies. The ministry of reconciliation is our Lord's triumph song.
>
> **DR. GLENN BURRIS**
> PRESIDENT, FOURSQUARE CHURCH

> *Mended* is truly an authentic story of how a couple's journey through tragedy brought redemption. Their story brings hope to any who are experiencing trauma in family relationships. Included in Rick and Tiffany's story is the narration of each of their children and how they are individually responding in this restorative process. Engaged or seasoned couples will glean insightful resources on how to safeguard their relationship and navigate healing in crisis. We highly recommend this book to all ministry couples!
>
> **JOHN AND MARTY WEBB**
> TRIAGECARE MINISTRY

TESTIMONIES

FROM AN UNFAITHFUL WIFE

❝ As a woman who had been unfaithful to my husband I felt broken beyond repair, and crumbled to dust with every ounce of my being. Reading *Mended*, I found myself able to relate to Tiffany in nearly every, heart-wrenching, emotional way. The emotions and experiences Tiffany conveyed were almost the complete description of the pain I was unable to describe in my own words. Tiffany portrays her journey from pain and isolation, not just from her family, but from God. She then captures her climb from the dark and heavy valley, to that of complete redemption—a new person, strengthened by the grace of God and the tools she used to help restore her shattered marriage. Reading *Mended* and witnessing God's mercy through Rick and Tiffany's journey has profoundly impacted my life, giving me a renewed hope for my marriage. While I still have a ways to go in dealing with my shame, *Mended* is a reference I'll return to. It's one reference I know Jesus wanted me to have.

C.L., WASHINGTON

FROM AN UNFAITHFUL HUSBAND

> Every man who is married or hopes to be married should read *Mended*. As a husband who sexually betrayed my spouse, I see how my careless words and actions watered the seeds of destruction that the devil tries to sow in every woman's soul. *Mended* takes you through the seemingly small neglects and hurts that every couple experiences to how the devil uses them to destroy a marriage. Rick and Tiffany clearly articulate the steps that they both took through Pure Desire's clinical program to restore their marriage and their family into a powerful example of what God wishes for every marriage.
>
> R.D., OREGON

A HUSBAND WHOSE WIFE WAS UNFAITHFUL

> *Mended* is a much-needed resource for those individuals, couples, and families devastated by betrayal and/or sexual addiction. In a world that had been turned upside down—where my heart was shattered to pieces, not trusting anything or anyone, filled with such deep woundedness, anger, resentment, anxiety, depression and despair—this book validated my feelings. In addition to a Christian-based recovery program, healing, redemption, and restoration for me, my wife, and our marriage, it gave me hope. Allowing God to work in our lives and believing that in him, all things are possible!
>
> P.C., SOUTH CAROLINA

A WIFE WHOSE HUSBAND WAS UNFAITHFUL

❝ *Mended* has something for everyone—the addict, the betrayed, married and engaged couples. If we identify what we bring from our family history into a marriage we can avoid a lot of unnecessary expectations and heartache. Rick and Tiffany identified their differences and were able to not only restore their marriage, but make it better than they ever imagined. God didn't give up on them. Their story is proof that God's mercy and grace can overcome Satan's attack on the institution of marriage.

M.D., OREGON

A DIVORCED SINGLE WOMAN

❝ *Mended* is a heartfelt story of redemption and grace that offers a window into the lives of an ordinary family with an extraordinary testimony. Through this book, they reveal the intimate ways in which God's abundant mercy and ability to heal, even the most devastating of circumstances, carried them to where they are today. Rick and Tiffany walk you through the story of their lives from their childhood beginnings to present day in such a way that you feel like you're just getting to know new friends over coffee. Through this journey, they share a deeply personal story of marital disconnect, painful wounding, and finally God's ultimate healing and restoration. *Mended* offers a raw and candid view of one couple's inspiring story that countless people can relate to, and find hope and encouragement in knowing that God is still in the business of doing miracles.

C.K., CALIFORNIA

A DIVORCED SINGLE WOMAN

❝ *Mended* is a story of heartbreak; how Rick and Tiffany Bulman coped while restoring their marriage and family. Their story reveals how misunderstandings and untruthfulness happen, and shows the importance of knowing your spouse's family history and their expectations before marriage. *Mended* is a narrative of the Bulmans' struggle to heal their family through prayer, faith, and counseling. You have a front row seat on how to negotiate 'feelings.' Their story is a testament to the power of the love and support of friends. This is a must-read for all and is an invaluable resource for those who search for answers.

M.W., WASHINGTON

A COUPLE SEPARATED AND RESTORED

❝ Reading the book *Mended* caused our thoughts to drift to our separation. Our sixth year of marriage we went to counseling and still separated for a year. I could have used Rick's journey to look at myself if I had read the book. My wife could identify with Tiffany and learned to talk out issues. Thank God we know Him and trusted Him to guide us.

S. AND M.P., FLORIDA

A SINGLE MAN

❝ Anyone who honestly wants to understand how God works His miracles each and every day would find the book *Mended* a courageous read in how God's love conquered. It is for those soon-to-be-married and those already married, so they can understand why loved ones do and say what they do. A top #1 read for a successful marriage!

C.A., WASHINGTON

HEALTHY COUPLES: HUSBAND

❝ Reading *Mended* was a blessing in my marriage. Rick and Tiffany's real-life story provides insights into how seemingly minor issues compounded over time can compromise what appears to be a strong marriage and nearly collapse it. Whether rock-solid or struggling just to hang on, I believe any couple will benefit from reading this story and the practical steps that accompany it in order to protect the integrity of the greatest earthly relationship that exists.

B.B., WASHINGTON

HEALTHY COUPLES: WIFE

❝ Rick and Tiffany's candid portrayal and stubborn clinging to God's grace inspired me. The practical tools they include strengthened me and guided me toward healing, reconciliation, and maturity in Christ for the long haul. *Mended* is a serious, in-depth look into two lives that could have gone so wrong, but instead shine forth the glory of God. The Apostle Paul said, 'Be imitators.' Rick and Tiffany have given us an example for the hard road to joyful marriage.

N.C., CANADA

HEALTHY COUPLES: HUSBAND AND WIFE

❝ My wife and I both read *Mended* and loved it! Rick and Tiffany took us on a journey through the pitfalls all married couples face—past hurts, broken dreams, selfishness, and our failure to trust God in the midst of it. They showed us how God can restore any marriage when two people are willing. Your marriage is definitely worth it and so is *Mended*.

D. AND S.D., CALIFORNIA

HEALTHY COUPLES: WIFE

❝ 'How could they do that?' Have you ever wonder this: when you hear a marriage you thought was perfect, is a casualty to adultery? Rick and Tiffany take us through that dark valley and offer hope to those who want their marriage to not just survive, but thrive. As a reader, I felt compelled to evaluate myself and ask where my blind spots are when I'm choosing myself over my spouse at the expense of him feeling loved. *Mended* is a powerful tool and a book of hope that God can redeem any marriage where hearts are willing to submit to Him.

K.R., WASHINGTON

HEALTHY COUPLES: WIFE

❝ *Mended* is a story of two broken people who took a situation our culture would look upon as destroyed and chose God's call to forgiveness and restoration. Rick and Tiffany tell a story that occurs all too often in marriage. They are transparent in their narrative of selfishness, disrespect, and the neglect of their primary relationship. I believe this book to be both a warning to spouses who may be falling into unhealthy patterns and a way to recognize and change course. It also serves as hope to those who have encountered a betrayal, that all is not lost and that Jesus has a perfect plan for healing in the most difficult of circumstances.

T.H., WASHINGTON

MENDED

ONE COUPLE'S JOURNEY
FROM BETRAYAL TO IMPERFECT BEAUTY

RICK AND TIFFANY BULMAN

MENDED

© Copyright Rick and Tiffany Bulman
Printed in the United States of America
ALL RIGHTS RESERVED
www.puredesire.org

Published by
Pure Desire Ministries International
www.puredesire.org | Gresham, Oregon | December 2018

ISBN 978-1-943291-71-7

No part of this publication may be reproduced, stored in a retrieval system, or transmitted in any form by any means—electronic, mechanical, photocopying, recording or otherwise—without prior written consent of Pure Desire Ministries International, except as provided by the United States of America copyright law.

Unless otherwise noted, all Scripture quotations are from THE HOLY BIBLE, NEW INTERNATIONAL VERSION®, NIV®. Copyright © 1973, 1978, 1984, 2011 by Biblica, Inc.®. Used by permission. All rights reserved worldwide.

Scripture quotations noted (KJV) are from the King James Version, which is in public domain.

Scripture quotations noted (NASB) are from the NEW AMERICAN STANDARD BIBLE®. Copyright © 1960, 1962, 1963, 1968, 1971, 1972, 1973, 1975, 1977, 1995 by The Lockman Foundation. Used by permission.

Scripture quotations noted (MSG) are from The Message. Copyright © 1993, 1994, 1995, 1996, 2000, 2001, 2002. Used by permission of NavPress Publishing Group.

Scripture quotations noted (GNT) are from the Good News Translation® (Today's English Version, Second Edition). Copyright © 1992 American Bible Society. All rights reserved.

Scripture quotations noted (NLT) are from the Holy Bible, New Living Translation. Copyright © 1996, 2004, 2015 by Tyndale House Foundation. Used by permission of Tyndale House Publishers, Inc., Carol Stream, Illinois 60188. All rights reserved.

Scripture quotations noted (NKJV) are from the New King James Version®. Copyright © 1982 by Thomas Nelson. Used by permission. All rights reserved.

Content editing by Heather Kolb

Cover design, interior design, and typesetting by Elisabeth Windsor

Cover photo of Rick and Tiffany by Casey Kasparian

CONTENTS

FOREWORD v

ACKNOWLEDGMENTS vii

WHY THIS BOOK WAS WRITTEN ix

INTRODUCTION xi

CHAPTER 1: TIFFANY'S BACKSTORY 1

CHAPTER 2: RICK'S BACKSTORY 11

CHAPTER 3: A NEW BEGINNING 23

CHAPTER 4: DING! FIGHTING IN THIS CORNER 35

CHAPTER 5: RICK'S MISTRESS 49

CHAPTER 6: THE BETRAYAL 61

CHAPTER 7: ROAD TO RECOVERY, PART 1 77

CHAPTER 8: ROAD TO RECOVERY, PART 2 89

CHAPTER 9: RETURNING TO THE CHURCH 103

CHAPTER 10: KALEB, JOSHUA, JARED, AND FAITH .. 117

CHAPTER 11: TIFFANY'S THOUGHTS 133

CHAPTER 12: RICK'S THOUGHTS 149

CHAPTER 13: EPILOGUE 163

CHAPTER 14: DISCOVERING THE RIGHT TOOLS ... 169

BIBLIOGRAPHY 187

FOREWORD

So many couples and church families are dealing with the devastating effects of moral failure in marriages—many churches today have no idea what to do or where to go for help. The church has typically responded in one of two extremes in dealing with moral failure. They either sweep everything under the carpet and the pastor is suddenly let go with no mention of a healing, restoration process; or, the more damaging option: the pastor is let go and the rumor mill kicks into high gear. Individuals take sides, and the couple and congregation are torn to pieces!

In this totally unique book, Rick and Tiffany share their courageous story of choosing to fight for the survival of their 20-year marriage; that by many estimations could never be revived. They knew that when people found out about the affair of their pastor's wife, the ripple effects would be like a tsunami that could destroy the lives of their family and their church.

Rick and Tiffany contacted Pure Desire Ministries and asked if we could help. Fortunately, their denomination and church family were open to us presenting a healing plan for the marriage and a possible restoration plan for them as pastors of their church. We will never forget the tension of the first congregational meeting, where we laid out what we hoped would be God's gracious plan for restoration for the marriage and flock.

Throughout this marvelous book, you have the opportunity to travel with Rick and Tiffany on the rollercoaster journey of facing their fears: dealing with their past accumulated pain, their fears of trusting each other, and uncovering wounds that caused their marriage to become toxic. During this process, they began to learn a beautiful new dance: one choreographed with steps of true authenticity, vulnerability, and trust.

Each of their four children share their story—how they individually processed the shock, shame, and wounds born out of a parent's infidelity. To our knowledge, there isn't another book on the market that has such candid statements shared by a couples' children. They each reveal their own gut-wrenching and challenging journey toward healing.

Rick and Tiffany share how difficult the journey was for many in their congregation. Tiffany gave the congregation a great gift by facing her fear of rejection through confession and repentance, with hope for restoration. There were those in the church who were unable to walk with them in this healing journey—for some, the betrayal was too deep.

But as Rick states, "'Our mess' has become our 'message.'" Those reading this book, who think their marriage is headed for a dead end, will gain hope for their own journey. Like Rick and Tiffany, they might discover a miraculous detour around that dead end and experience the scandalous love of a redeeming God.

Words can never express how deeply proud we are of Rick and Tiffany. They have displayed such courage and humility. They have given other couples, who may be caught in the hell of adultery and betrayal, a powerful picture of hope and healing.

Their story is proof that there is:

- no wound Christ can't heal,
- no tragedy Christ can't transform,
- and no marriage Christ can't make new!

DR. TED ROBERTS AND DIANE ROBERTS

ACKNOWLEDGMENTS

We are incredibly grateful for the many people who not only stood by our side, but were actively involved and used instrumentally to help bring healing and wholeness to our marriage and family.

First and foremost we are humbled and filled with such gratitude to our King Jesus! Thank you, Lord, for ferociously loving us and speaking directly into our spirit. You were and are the glue that binds us together as a couple and family!

Thank you to all our immediate and extended family. You did not JUDGE us but rather LOVED us. Your commitment to our well-being by daily walking alongside us, being very active through your words, your financial support, and merely making yourself present, gave us the footing we needed to redeem our marriage and family. Having you in our corner played an instrumental part in our success. We love you all so much!

We want to thank Dr. Ted and Diane Roberts of Pure Desire Ministries. You both were a divine appointment for us. Very literally we found hope and promise for our marriage because of your love, guidance, and expertise. You cried with us, laughed with us, and brought much-needed correction, all the while cheering us on through encouraging words. Your impact has revolutionized the way we do life together as a couple and family. THANK YOU!

We are thankful to all our Foursquare family who came alongside us and spoke hope and healing into our lives. Due to the confidentiality of this book, we cannot mention you by name, but you all know who you are. We love you and value your ongoing friendship and support.

Thank you Sue Miholer, for your editorial wisdom. Not only did you help clean up our words, but you went the extra mile and graciously explained literary rules along the way. You are a gem!

Thank you, William Johnson, for being a friend and sounding board for the many creative ideas of the *Mended* project. You are a good man!

Thank you to our church family, you know who you are—you stood by us and endured the heartache and most importantly, the redemption side of our marriage and family. We will always love you!

With much gratitude we extend a warm thank you to: Jeff, Judy, Kristen, Dave, Russ, Casey, Brant, Margaret, Chuck, Bob, Dorene; all who were a part of our focus group—for your love, wisdom and advice in caring for us and sharing your thoughts on how to best tell our story in a way that will minister to others. Getting your collective wisdom directly shaped how this book was written.

A special thanks to Jon M., Dan D. and Tawnya, and Misael H. for immediately being there the night all hell broke loose, and shortly after. Your listening ears, hospitality, prayers, and encouraging words saved us in the darkest hour of our life. Your friendship is valued beyond words.

Thank you, John and Marty Webb, for your friendship and support. We greatly appreciate you both. Thank you, Marty, for the "Heart Check" sections at the end of every chapter. They are a valuable contribution to this work. We love you!

And to the Pure Desire staff who helped creatively and logistically put our story into book form, thank you! Your partnership means the world to us!

WHY THIS BOOK WAS WRITTEN

The vision behind writing *Mended* started out as a letter to our children to help them avoid the pitfalls we fell into. We wanted to give them an overview of our relationship that would serve as what not to do and, eventually what to do, in hopes they would learn from our mistakes and understand the Lord's victory in our marriage and family.

Our family suffered a traumatic experience. Writing our story for our kids was not meant to give excuses, but instead to provide a greater context to what led to the betrayal that took place.

As our book began to take shape, we recognized it could be used as a testimony to help people who are going through a similar experience, as well as be a general resource for couples and pre-marrieds.

Mended will cause individuals and couples to examine themselves and their relationships for the greater good. It will serve as a testimony of the healing that can take place between two people when they give the Lord willing hearts to work with.

Mended is not a technical book on the "how-tos" of mending a broken marriage, directly. There are many amazing books on the market that give in-depth practical steps (the how-tos) that can serve singles and couples on multiple levels. You'll find a list in the bibliography.

Mended is a testimony of our lives—a personal account starting with our childhoods and continuing through our meeting each other, getting married, and then exposing our inability to get on the same page for so long that it played a part in the betrayal that took place. Fortunately, the story doesn't end there. The reader gets to journey with us through the tough work of our recovery that restored our marriage and family.

We believe our story can help safeguard people from making the same mistakes we did.

Lastly, we encourage you not to skip the introduction of this book, which lays the foundation for what you are about to read. It will provide a context that will benefit the reader as you journey through our story. The introduction will serve as a bookmark that will help you connect the dots along the way.

Blessings to you as you read, *Mended: One Couple's Journey from Betrayal to Imperfect Beauty*.

OUR FAMILY...
PLEASE TAKE A MOMENT AND NOTICE OUR HAPPY FAMILY!

INTRODUCTION

We want to thank you for taking the time to read our story. We are humbled at the opportunity to be able to share it with you. Our prayer is that our journey will bring insight, encouragement and, most importantly, hope in the midst of a situation that may feel hopeless.

The photos on the previous page are of our tribe. We look like a typical fun, happy family. We have four kids, and we are all comfortable being goofy with one another. We will even take the time to modify a picture by putting a frame around it while adding the word LOVE to post it for the world to see on social media. However, what you are seeing was not an *accurate representation* of the reality that was present.

During the time that each one of these photos was taken, a deep dark secret of betrayal laid hidden beneath the surface. The fun, happy-go-lucky family—from the outside looking in—seemed great. But behind closed doors, we were very dysfunctional.

This is our story. On the one hand, it tells of misfortune, hardship, and tragedy. On the other, it is a testimony of love, commitment, mercy, and grace. You will witness innocent naïveté coupled with our natural tendency to be humanly selfish. You, the reader, will feel like a bystander looking in on our marriage and family from the outside as you watch the makings of a train wreck that is about to happen.

We want to be transparent with our struggles, failures, and the betrayal that came so close to destroying our family. Our story is written *intentionally* in a *conversational manner* because we want you, the reader, to feel like you're sitting in our living room with us as we take turns sharing our life and marriage experiences in the succinct order in which we lived it out. Everything we share is what led up to the reason this book is written.

Before getting married, we were naïve about the amount of baggage we would bring into our union. It was lost on us that our growing-up years would have the impact they did. They shaped our views about life, marriage, raising children, etc. Such viewpoints were now going to be a part of each other's daily reality, which eventually caused friction that led to intense arguing, emotional abuse, neglect, and ultimately an affair.

One of the biggest mistakes we made was that we never considered what we had witnessed and experienced as children would manifest in negative ways and cause damage to our relationship. We had blinders on and thought we would live happily ever after.

Genesis 2:24 says, "Therefore shall a man leave his father and his mother, and shall cleave unto his wife: and they shall be one flesh" (KJV). Tiffany and I did not know what that verse truly meant, although we thought we did. A successful leaving and cleaving requires a pledge, a covenant between a newly married couple that their past familiar way of doing things would be replaced with new loyalties based on new priorities—*each other*.

For many years in our marriage, we were not leaving and cleaving. From our childhood, we naturally took what we had learned and perceived as the way to do certain things and made them law in our hearts and minds. The big mistake about doing this was we never took the time to share our convictions about how a specific something should be accomplished, handled, or carried out. This would lead to many frustrating moments because when the other person violated what we believed to be true, we got angry and sometimes reacted toward each other as if an actual sin had been committed.

We wish we had learned before getting married what Drs. Les and Leslie Parrott have coined in their book, *Saving Your Marriage Before It Starts*, as "unspoken rules."[1] Unspoken rules are expectations one spouse does not realize they have, while the other spouse is entirely unaware of the rule's existence. The unspoken rule typically reveals itself when one spouse violates the other's internal conviction of how a particular something should be done. It is unspoken because the one spouse has never explained to the other what they feel should be a rule or way of doing something based on various beliefs and reasons: such as a household duty or how Christmas morning should be celebrated.

We came to learn that a lot of arguments between married couples could be headed off at the pass if both people in the relationship realized the truth about the existence of unspoken rules. They could have "ah-ha" moments, halt the conversation, and say, "Hey, I think we're encountering an unspoken rule. Let's dialogue about why you (or I) feel so strongly about *(fill in the blank)*. Where is this convicting feeling or thought to do *(fill in the blank)* coming from?"

As a couple, if we had understood the existence of unspoken rules, maybe we would have noticed when we experienced such occurrences. Hopefully, we would have been mature enough to realize we were just having differing opinions rather than the idea that the other person was trying to be *rebellious* or *inconsiderate* toward the other. Had we been aware, maybe we would have chosen at that moment to leave and cleave—cleaving by re-

---

1. Parrott, L. & Parrott, L. (2006). *Saving Your Marriage Before It Starts: Seven Questions to Ask Before—and After—You Marry*. Grand Rapids, MI: Zondervan.

creating a new way or new rule about how we do something based on our pledge, our covenant of doing life together. As you read on, we'll highlight when we fell into this trap.

Since unspoken rules played a significant part in our disagreements, we strategically decided to begin our story by *not* jumping ahead to the couple of years prior to the affair; instead it is helpful to provide a little historical overview of our lives.

The first and second chapters are our backstories, and the third chapter is the beginning of our lives colliding. It's necessary to get a glimpse into our growing-up and early-married years. The insight you'll gain will give you an advantage in being able to begin connecting the dots as you read on, which will allow you to see the possible outcome even before we did.

As you read our story, you'll see that our lack of understanding of one another and also ourselves caused unnecessary strife. This tension we created between us, albeit normal at times, was used by the enemy to stir the pot of division in our marriage.

Peppered throughout our story, and specifically in the later chapters, are many moral and biblical truths we learned while on our journey to recovery and reconciliation.

At the end of each chapter are sets of questions. These questions are designed for *reflection* on and *connection* to the material just read. They will help the reader begin to process their own life in light of our story. Our goal is to help bring to light any familiarity the reader may have to what we have gone through. We encourage processing these questions with a counselor or third party.

We also discovered *practical* everyday tools that helped rescue us from the dark path we were on. We hope you can glean the lessons we learned, as well as implement the tools that proved to be lifesavers for us. Our heart is to prevent others from getting caught in the same vicious cycle we did.

INTRODUCTION

Simply put, we want to make our *mess* our *message*. We hope our story will safeguard you (and your spouse) from experiencing the same pitfalls we did, which almost cost us our marriage and family. Our prayer is that you will read this story with eyes to see, ears to hear, and a heart opened to learn from our mistakes. We desire that you learn from the steps we took *to* and *through* recovery and to what we now call *imperfect beauty*. We see our marriage that way because it is far from perfect, but because of the grace of God and His *ongoing* restorative work in our lives, it is beautiful in an *imperfect* sanctifying way.

BLESSINGS TO YOU AS YOU ARE ON YOUR JOURNEY!
RICK AND TIFFANY

CHAPTER 1

TIFFANY'S BACKSTORY
I HAVE AN ANGEL WATCHING OVER ME; I CALL HIM DADDY

I was born in the spring of 1969 on a beautiful sunny Wednesday morning at 8:32 a.m. in the town of San Leandro, California. From what I was told, and choose to believe, my parents were filled with immense joy. I am the oldest child in my family. I have an amazing sister and brother whom I love dearly.

Early in my childhood, my parents decided to move to the Pacific Northwest to start a business. The company did well in the small community we called home. It afforded my family a decent living, giving us the freedom to purchase a home, go on vacations, and enjoy certain comforts of life.

When I was five years old, my family accepted Christ, and we began attending a church in our local community. As I grew up, we became an intricate part of our church family. My sister and I sang on the worship team. When my brother got older, he joined the team as the new drummer. Life was good as we became more a part of our community and church. We were and still are a tight family who genuinely enjoys each other's company.

When my dad came home from work, my mom had dinner ready, and we always ate as a family. These were times I cherished. We laughed as each one of us shared how our day went. I remember the evening my mom hid a tape recorder while we ate dinner to capture the conversation taking place. After dinner, she brought out dessert and revealed what she had done. We all died laughing as we listened to the dinner conversation. These moments as a family helped build the closeness and camaraderie we have today.

My dad was very detailed oriented, something I learned from him. He had this awareness and took note of things some people may blow off. One of the cutest memories I have is when he made our lunches for school. He noticed if we didn't have a dessert, and took the time to put butter between graham crackers to give us something sweet to eat. He was thorough and lovingly quirky that way.

His awareness was not only about if we had or didn't have something. He also caught the smallest changes in a room. If a light bulb burned out, he noticed immediately and changed it. If something had been cleaned, he always remarked on it quickly. If a new picture was hung on a wall, or a chair was moved to the other side of the room, immediately after entering the room he would comment on it. "Hey, that's different," he'd point out.

If I had cleaned my room, he always came in and said, "Your room looks nice." Or, if I had straightened up the bathroom, he'd mention how tidy the bathroom looked, and that he knew I cleaned it. It always made me feel good that he noticed my hard work.

As I grew older, I came to appreciate people's recognition. I like things clean, and if someone recognized my work, there was an additional sense of satisfaction that came with what I had done.

As a teenager, it always brought me comfort when I saw my dad taking care of our family. Almost every Saturday, I saw

CHAPTER I: TIFFANY'S BACKSTORY

him washing all of our car windows and checking the oil—my parent's car, my car, and my sister's. It was commonplace to find him tending to the yard, taking care of the house, and always going around at night making sure all doors and windows were locked before our family went to bed. Looking back on those fond memories, I remember feeling safe; I felt loved and cared for.

My dad was not just always there for our family, but also personally for me. I knew if something needed attention, he would always come through. When looking back on my childhood, I can see where my main love languages were cultivated. In Dr. Gary Chapman's book, *The Five Love Languages: How to Express Heartfelt Commitment to Your Mate*, he outlines five ways to express and experience love, which Chapman calls "Love Languages"— Receiving Gifts, Quality Time, Words of Affirmation, Acts of Service (Devotion), and Physical Touch.[2]

MY THREE MAIN LOVE LANGUAGES ARE:

- **Acts of Service:** The husbandly duties my dad performed caring for the household produced a sense of being loved and valued.
- **Gifts:** The kind gestures from my parents made me feel thought of and appreciated.
- **Quality Time:** Family time and being asked how my day went made me feel valued.

These little experiences along the way that I had in my childhood shaped me. And, as a little girl who fantasized about her future

---

2. Chapman, G. (1995). *The Five Love Languages: How to Express Heartfelt Commitment to Your Mate.* Chicago, IL: Northfield Publishing.

husband, I naturally thought every guy would be like my dad. As you continue to read our story, you will see that Rick, not knowing what my love languages were, spoke only *his* love languages, which is a common mistake for couples. This caused serious issues for us. I did not realize through my misinterpretation of his intentions or lack thereof that I resented him for something he was not aware of. My misunderstanding played a part in causing division in our marriage.

Things were not always hunky-dory in my childhood household. We had normal—and at times, not so normal—issues that needed to be dealt with. We had our fair share of struggles. My parents were like every other parent, imperfect people trying to raise imperfect children. Their upbringing played a part in how they ran our household, which caused the normal tension a family experiences from time to time.

My mom was raised not to show any emotion. If she expressed herself negatively, she was punished. She vowed not to raise her children that way and would allow them to express their feelings—within reason, of course. I had a very tenacious personality and was independent and strong-willed. I often pushed the boundaries when expressing my frustration, as well as allowing my temper to get the better of me. I had an anger problem that had been passed down from generation to generation. I never dealt with my anger growing up and therefore took it into my marriage with Rick. Looking back, I wish I had gone to the Lord for healing in this area since it did cause tension between the two of us and our children.

My siblings and I, as much as we loved one another, argued as we got older. Being the eldest child in the family, I was called upon to watch my sister and brother when my parents were gone. When we were home alone with each other, I'd lose my temper when they did not do what I wanted.

CHAPTER 1: TIFFANY'S BACKSTORY

As the oldest, I did not like being teased, being made fun of, or not taken seriously. I found it disrespectful and rude. In those moments, the fight in *fight or flight* kicked in.[3] I could be quick-witted and combative and tried to get the last word. As I was growing up, my anger often got the best of me. From time to time, I'd slam my bedroom door and yell in my room, as well as being sarcastic to my parents face to face. This behavior often landed me in trouble.

As a pre-teen to a teenager, I was not confident. I was kind of nerdy and just liked to read. Even though I was a cheerleader my senior year of high school, I never played sports. I stuck to reading and singing in the choir. Most of my growing-up years, I did not hang out with the cool kids who wore the cool clothes. I felt my parents were too strict. In some cases, they may have been too strict, but looking back, overall, what I interpreted as strict was called "parenting"—something I would learn more about later on in life.

However, I was not allowed to do certain things, and in my mind I felt like I didn't have a sense of control. The rebellious side of me would kick in and create opportunities to have control. One way I tried to control things was through an eating disorder I developed sometime between my sophomore and junior year of high school.

Looking back on that time in my life, I didn't see myself as overweight. I was skinny and knew it. To me, not eating was something I could control. Every morning I'd have an Instant Breakfast but then throw my lunch away, which I felt guilty about doing. My parents did not allow me to do certain things, but

---

3. Roberts, D. (2010). *Pure Desire for Women: Eight Pillars to Freedom from love addiction & sexual issues*. Gresham, OR: Pure Desire Ministries International.

eating or not eating was something I could control when I was away from home.

I never really did things that were horrific, serious offenses. I never drank, never did drugs, never went to parties or got in trouble with the law. I was pretty boring in that regard. The worst thing I did was being sneaky at times. I hid small makeup compacts because I was not allowed to wear makeup when my friends started. I hid what I had and put it on at school, but made sure to take it off before I came home. The level of my crazy rebellious ways went only as far as having a friend bring nylons to school so I could wear them since I was not allowed to at that time.

I eventually graduated from high school and started attending the local community college while working at Safeway, our town's main grocery store. Because I was involved in children's ministry at our church, I developed a connection with kids, which instilled in me a desire to want to pursue something in child development. But, like most newly graduated high schoolers, I had no clue what that would look like for me. So, attending the local college to get my general education out of the way made sense.

One day after coming home from a Sunday evening service, my mom gave me a L.I.F.E. Bible College pamphlet she had picked up in the church foyer. I looked it over and moments later told her that I'd like to look into going to this school. The timing could not have been better. My best friend Jodi was moving to California at the end of the summer to attend the following semester at Azusa Pacific University, which is near L.I.F.E. Bible College. This helped in making my decision to move down south with Jodi.

Jodi and I made it safe and sound to our respective schools. We got acclimated to a new area, new schedules, and new friends. Every Sunday, Jodi and I met up to go to her parent's house. They had moved down with her to pastor a church in Hesperia,

CHAPTER 1: TIFFANY'S BACKSTORY

California. We grew up singing together and often sang duets on Sunday mornings; I miss those times with her.

One Sunday, as I was on the platform, I looked out into the congregation and saw a handsome young man. He was about six feet tall and thinly built with brown hair, blue eyes, and sideburns that accented his facial features. I asked Jodi, "Who is the guy that looks like one of those actors from the TV show Beverly Hills 90210? He's cute."

"His name is Rick," Jodi told me. I asked her to introduce me to him.

HEART CHECK

...he [God] guarded him [them] as the apple of his eye.
DEUTERONOMY 32:10

// 1. Describe your relationship with:

Your mom.

_____
_____
_____
_____

Your dad.

_____
_____
_____
_____

Your siblings.

_____
_____
_____
_____

// 2. Was your childhood home life a safe environment?

I felt safe because:

_____
_____
_____
_____

I felt unsafe because:

_____
_____
_____
_____

// 3. Was your childhood home life a place of security?

I felt secure when:

_____
_____
_____
_____

I did not feel secure when:

_____
_____
_____
_____

// 4. What were tangible ways you felt "loved and cherished" with your parent(s) or guardian(s)?

_____
_____
_____
_____
_____
_____
_____
_____

// 5. List some "unspoken rules" you experienced in your family of origin—things that seemed like there was only one way to do or say things.

_____
_____
_____
_____
_____
_____
_____
_____
_____

CHAPTER 2

RICK'S BACKSTORY
SOLD THROUGH LOVE; BOUGHT THROUGH LOVE

I was born in the spring of 1971, to Tony and Kathi Drago in Long Beach, California. The name given to me was Anthony Alfred Drago, and for the first seven years of my life, I went by Little Tony. My dad worked for Hughes Market, running their seafood department, and my mother was a stay-at-home mom. My parents were two newly married young twenty-somethings living day-to-day, paycheck-to-paycheck. Over the next few years, they grew apart and decided to divorce when I was three years old. I was fortunate to have my dad stay in my life, for which I am truly grateful.

About a year later my mom met a man by the name of Rick Bulman. Rick was a Marine Corps sergeant in his mid-twenties, who, after spending time fighting in Vietnam was honorably discharged. He and my mom's relationship grew quickly and they ended up getting married in Las Vegas. I suddenly found myself with another dad. It was something I had to get used to as he looked and acted nothing like my biological father, Tony. Shortly after getting married, my mom and stepdad, Rick, found

Jesus and committed to living for Him and raised our family in a Christian home with biblical values.

When I was in the first grade, we moved to the high desert, Adelanto, California, and then eventually moved to Victorville a few miles away. At the time, these were small safe communities. We never locked our doors or windows at night. In fact, I remember my dad Rick always left the key in the ignition of the green truck that he parked in our front yard. At that time, the worst thing about the desert was the tumbleweed in the yard and dust storms. It was rare to wash our car because it got dirty immediately.

One day, when I was seven, my dad Tony called my mom and asked if Rick could adopt me so he and his new wife wouldn't have to pay child support.

My mom was surprised and asked Rick what he thought. Deep down inside, Rick had always wanted to adopt me, so he jumped at the chance and told my mom, "Tell Tony yes! And, he doesn't have to wait until the adoption is final to stop paying child support; he can stop paying the $140 as of today." My dad (Tony) agreed.

Rick was excited at this opportunity; it was important to him to do this. He wanted to show his love and commitment to me as my father. Rick wanted me to know he didn't see me as a *stepson* but as his *actual* son. When he and my mom shared the news, they both made it clear that Tony would always be recognized and respected as my father and would continue to have uninterrupted access to me.

Sometime later, after Rick agreed to the adoption, a social worker came to the house to sit down and interview him and my mom, along with me. This gentleman needed to make sure I understood what was going to take place.

At the end of the meeting, *without* talking with my parents, the social worker looked in my direction and asked, "Now that

CHAPTER 2: RICK'S BACKSTORY

Rick is going to adopt you, would you like to change your name?" The oxygen immediately left the room since everyone was shocked by this question.

My mom chimed in immediately, "Change his name? What do you mean change his name? He can do that?" The social worker replied, "Of course he can."

And then again, he looked at me and asked, "So, do you want to?" Being young and stunned, my parents didn't know what to do. Should they tell the social worker no or just go with it?

I piped up immediately and said, "Heck yeah! I can be anyone I want?" The social worker said, "Technically, yes, if Rick and your mom approve of your choice of name."

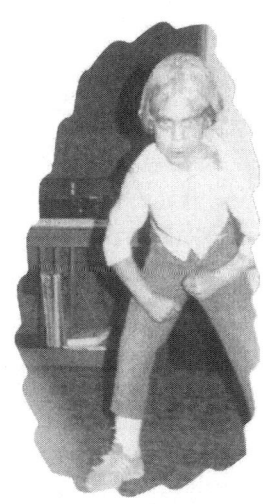

"I've got it! I know what I want my new name to be!" Everyone in the room leaned forward on the edge of their seats, stunned that I had come up with something so quickly. "What is it?" they asked in unison.

"THE INCREDIBLE HULK!" I shouted seriously. They all laughed and told me to pick a real name and not a character. I thought for a moment. "How about Harold?"

My parents laughed, but the social worker didn't. "What's so funny about the name Harold?" he asked. "Harold is his little friend from down the street," my mom replied. "We can be Harolds together!" I protested. The social worker laughed. "Well, I'll leave this up to you and your parents to decide."

In the end, I went from Anthony Alfred Drago to Glenn Richmond Bulman III, but I went by Rick(y). Years later, when I was 16, I asked my mom, "Why did my dad Tony give me up for adoption?" My mom *very carefully* responded, "Hon, it was not a heart decision, but a financial decision. His wife wanted for them to stop paying child support."

She went on and told me it was more of a paper transaction versus a father not wanting his son. Even though I believed her because my dad *never* stopped being in my life, I still kind of felt like I had been sold for a measly $140 per month savings.

Growing up, I was convinced my dad Tony did love me because he still came to a lot of my sporting events; he never missed a birthday or Christmas and came to see me all the time. When he said he was going to do something, he did it. I was and am still blessed to have him a part of my life. However, one day when I was 18 years old, I confronted him about his decision to ask Rick to adopt me.

With sorrow in his eyes, he said, "It's the number one regret in my life. I allowed my wife to talk me into it. I wanted to keep the peace with her, so I agreed. I should have stood my ground and told her no. It's not her fault, but ultimately mine for saying yes."

Although the subject of my adoption rarely comes up, when it does my dad Tony always says with pain in his voice, "I wish I had never done that. I should have stood up to my ex-wife."

Growing up I loved sports and played just about anything I could get my hands on. I was a hyper child without an off button. Even though I was being raised in the church and loved Jesus to

CHAPTER 2: RICK'S BACKSTORY

the degree that a child could, I was a handful. I got into trouble in school and at home quite frequently.

It was common for me to find myself on restriction and made to do yard work for long periods of time. I hated yard work! I grew to resent doing it since it was one of the tools-of-choice for a punishment. Unfortunately, it took many years into our marriage before I finally set aside my childish mindset (i.e., grew up), stopped procrastinating, and started caring for our home(s) in that way.

I was the eldest sibling and loved to be right. I had a quick-witted personality, and if sarcasm was a gift, I possessed and functioned in it. However, my teasing or ridicule could be mean-spirited, so it often landed me in trouble. What's interesting is that this type of behavior was not modeled for me. Growing up, I never heard or saw my parents argue. They were never demeaning or cutting with their words; they were masters at hiding their conflict. This was something I always admired about them. However, my sarcasm and cutting words were tools I used out of insecurity to make me feel better about myself.

Years later, I realized why I functioned this way. At the time, I did not understand why my punishments were harsher. I failed to comprehend that they were because of the degree to which I broke the rule. Being the oldest child in our family by five and nine years, my mistakes were always far worse. For example, at age eight, I spray-painted the side of a barn. I was spanked and put on restriction. My sister Jennifer, at age three, took a toy from our one-year-old sister Stephanie, which made her cry.

"Jennifer, no, no. You don't take the toy from Stephanie. Give it back and say you're sorry," my parents told her.

I'd hear that and think, "All she gets is a 'no, no?' Shoot, I would have gotten spanked and put on restriction," which I would not have, but in my eight-year-old mind, I saw it that way.

What could not be further from the truth was that I viewed my punishments in comparison to those given my siblings as *unfair*; therefore, I felt disconnected from everyone and not as loved by my parents. Plus, I visited my dad Tony, and because I didn't live with him, I felt I wasn't a complete member of his household.

In short, I grew up feeling like a kid without his own family, when in reality I had one. What's unfortunate is that I could not get myself to see that I was a part of a family. Because of my misinterpretation growing up, my insecurity and deep-seated jealousy of my half-siblings often got the best of me. My teasing or winning an argument would kick in, which was just a dishonest way of making me feel better about myself—even if it was at their expense.

Often my dad asked me to watch him fix various things around our house, change a tire, or hang something on the wall for my mom. He said that he needed to teach me to fix things because someday I would need to do so for my own family. I'd get bored because I just watched rather than participate in the task at hand.

When I asked if I could do something, the typical response was, in an encouraging tone, "Just watch; you'll learn."

However, he did not realize that I, like most people, learned by doing not by watching. I would ask questions like, "Can't you do it this way?" Or "What would happen if you did this?" It was my way of trying to contribute. More often than not, his response was, "No, just watch. You'll learn," and then he would continue to fix the object.

I eventually became very insecure about my mechanical abilities because I felt my ideas were always wrong. With that said, it was never my dad's intent to make me feel the way I did. As a child, I misinterpreted the heart of what was being said, and therefore, I

CHAPTER 2: RICK'S BACKSTORY

built a false narrative around my misunderstanding (i.e., I must not be smart enough, and that's why he just tells me to watch.)

I always saw my dad, Rick Sr., as an extremely hard worker. In my mind, he was *and still is* a machine. He always talked about the importance of having a good work ethic, to never cut corners, but always choose to do the right thing over what might be easiest or most comfortable. He worked long hours and sometimes his work carried into the evening while at home. When I was 16 to 18 years old, his job as a traveling salesman took him on the road during most of the week and home on the weekends for six months out of the year. However, he always seemed to make it a priority to attend my football games or any other sporting event I was involved in.

Due to his work schedule and seasons of traveling, I witnessed my mom running the household. She cooked, cleaned, did the laundry, gave kids baths, put them all to bed, chauffeured them around, handed out punishments, etc. This shaped my thinking: *the man works, and the wife runs the home.* It worked smoothly from what I could tell as a young boy growing up in that environment.

At the age of 19, I no longer lived at home. I had an unfulfilling job at a glass plant in Victorville. I felt disconnected from God and lost when I thought about my future. One day I needed some advice, and I went to my parent's house to ask them what I should do. My mom's response was, "Have you prayed about it? What do you think God is telling you?"

They always pointed me to the Lord to try to hear for myself what He had to say concerning my problems. I understood why she responded that way and didn't just tell me what she thought I should do. She was training me to learn to seek the Lord first and hear what He was saying, rather than stay in the habit of coming to them. As an adult, this was something I needed to learn: *seek God first.*

I left that conversation feeling frustrated. I just wanted my parents to tell me what to do. Asking God, whom I could not hear audibly, just seemed to be the slow way to get my answer. At that moment I had an epiphany. I thought, "Wow, I'm no longer living at home, and I can't keep running to my parents as an initial knee-jerk response when I need advice. I can either do life on my own or try to learn to listen and recognize God's voice and do life with Him."

It was at that moment, with tears streaming down my face, I cried out to the Lord and rededicated my life. I immediately made an inward commitment to not only attend church but also serve in any way I could. I vowed to follow the Lord and say yes to whatever He asked of me, although, I had no clue what that commitment would require—especially 23 years later.

Shortly after my church involvement began, our congregation received a new senior pastor. The family was a transplant from a church in the Pacific Northwest. This man's teaching was solid, edifying, and the worship ushered you right into the presence of God.

One Sunday morning, two young women sang a special song before the sermon. I remember seeing Tiffany for the first time and thinking, "Who is that beauty with the angelic voice singing with the pastor's daughter?"

After the church service, I made my way to the front to get a closer look at her. To my surprise, Jodi, Tiffany's best friend, approached me and said, "Hey, I want to introduce you to someone. Rick, this is Tiffany. Tiffany, this is Rick." I was floored; I didn't expect to be introduced to her. With nerves on high alert, I chatted with Tiffany and found out she was a L.I.F.E. Bible College student, the very school I wanted to attend the following fall semester to pursue my call to ministry.

CHAPTER 2: RICK'S BACKSTORY

Tiffany and I eventually became an item. We grew to love each other quickly and found that we had common goals. We both grew up in Christian homes, shared the same biblical values, and both of us desired to get married and have a family in the future. Just four short months after dating, I could not take it anymore and proposed to her. I was the happiest 21-year-old on earth when she said yes. The two of us set a date for the wedding that was exactly seven days before our one-year anniversary of dating.

We began premarital counseling, and as time grew closer to the wedding, we made an appointment to go to our pastor's home to outline the wedding service. Lots of conversation went back and forth between our pastor and us.

Suddenly, our pastor looked at me and said, "Let me ask you something. Does adultery necessitate divorce?" I remember thinking, "That's an odd random question." After a few seconds, I said, "No, adultery doesn't necessitate divorce, but it is biblical grounds for it."

"You're correct, Rick." Our pastor went on, "To say that it necessitates divorce is, in a way saying, that God is not big enough to heal and restore a marriage."

That was it; we did not speak any more on that topic. It was an odd and out-of-the-blue question. After that, the conversation continued to ebb and flow in various directions. However, it was a distinct part of our discussion the Holy Spirit would use years later to remind me of my answer.

HEART CHECK

For You created my inmost being; You knit me together in my mother's womb. I praise You because I am fearfully and wonderfully made; Your works are wonderful, I know that full well.

PSALM 139:13–14

// 1. Describe how your growing-up years shaped how you feel about yourself today.

_____
_____
_____
_____
_____
_____
_____
_____
_____
_____
_____
_____
_____
_____

// 2. Describe if and how you felt loved and accepted.

// 3. Describe any rejection you experienced as a child either at home, school, or with friends.

// **4. If and when you felt rejection, what did you do to cope (work, eat, smoke, drink, drugs, Internet)?**

_____
_____
_____
_____
_____
_____
_____
_____
_____
_____

// **5. Circle the words that applied to you as a child:**

- Inferior
- Lonely
- Peaceful
- Workaholic
- Helpless
- Fearful
- Confident
- Angry
- Loving
- Sad
- Mistrusting
- Anxious
- Insecure
- Joyful
- Hostile
- Hopeful
- Secure
- Forgiving

Other: _____
_____
_____

CHAPTER 3

A NEW BEGINNING
WHEN OPPOSITES ATTRACT

RICK: February 19, 1993 was a cold, very wet rainy Friday, and the storm continued to come in with a fierce vengeance. I was worried that nobody would attend our wedding the next day because conditions were so severe and seemingly getting worse. My dad Tony and I made it to the church for the rehearsal. In spite of the ugly conditions outside, everybody was excited and ready to partner with Tiffany and me in taking our next step of becoming husband and wife. Like a typical wedding rehearsal, there was humor, tears of joy, and nervousness as it settled into the minds of everyone that two families were becoming one in less than 24 hours.

That evening I kissed Tiffany goodnight, knowing that the next time I saw her would be when she walked down the aisle. My best man, John Driscoll, and I left with the rest of my groomsmen to stay at a mutual friend's house. I noticed that the storm was getting worse. The forecast predicted the wind to be heavy through the weekend, and I believed it as tree branches seem to be falling on the roads equally as often as the rain itself.

I prayed silently, "God, I have a weird request. If You can make the sun stand still, can You please, I beg of You, make the rain stop for tomorrow? After that, feel free to let it rain as much as You'd like!" Knowing that was a long shot of a prayer, I chuckled as I threw it God's way.

The next morning, I jumped out of bed and went to the window. Much to my surprise there were blue skies and bright sun illuminating everything. I ran outside and did a 360° turn in the driveway. I saw dark gray clouds in the distance *surrounding* Victorville. It was as if they were waiting for permission to converge on the small town. With sunny blue skies in the center of the dark gray ring of clouds, I simply thanked the Lord and accepted it as His sweet gift to Tiffany and me on our special day.

The wedding was flawless. There was laughter, special intimate moments, tears of joy—and most importantly, nobody fainted. The pastor turned us around to face our friends and family and said, "It is my privilege to introduce to you for the first time, Mr. and Mrs. Rick and Tiffany Bulman." Everyone cheered in loud applause as we made our way down the aisle toward the foyer of the church.

After the honeymoon, we returned to Tiffany's apartment, where she was a manager of a complex for a local corporation that owned more than 20 complexes in the area. It was a spacious four-bedroom apartment in West Covina, California, plenty of room for her and me. We were happy and still reeling from the reality that we were now married and were living together. I was working at a local restaurant as a waiter, as well as serving as the youth pastor in our church in Azusa, California.

Like all newlywed couples, we had to learn how to live with one another. Even though we grew up in households that shared the same Christian values, we were both uniquely made, wired differently, and were heavily influenced by how we were raised. This was a recipe for conflict, but a conflict that could be resolved, as we had to learn what it meant to *leave* and *cleave* to each other.

CHAPTER 3: A NEW BEGINNING

TIFFANY: A couple weeks into being married and living together, I noticed that Rick seemed to be in a bad mood as he dusted the entertainment center in our living room. I quickly picked up on his attitude, as he huffed and puffed and sighed while he cleaned. I finally asked him, "What's wrong?"

To my surprise, he fired back, "It's a Tuesday evening, and I don't want to be cleaning the apartment!"

"Then why are you?"

Rick went on to explain that he was cleaning because he saw me cleaning and felt he shouldn't just sit around and watch TV or do nothing. I let him know that, as much as I appreciated his help, I did not expect him to do anything. I told him I loved cleaning and straightening things up since it was my way of getting prepared for the next day. I told him to sit down and stop dusting and do whatever he felt like doing.

Within a week or so of being back from our honeymoon, I was frustrated and felt the need to scour the sink after Rick did the dinner dishes. He asked me what I was doing. "I'm scouring the sink," I said with an annoyed tone. Confused, he asked me why.

"You're supposed to scour the sink after you do the dinner dishes," I said as if it were a life rule and everyone was aware of it except him.

Suddenly the little Ricky Bulman in my husband appeared and asked, "What do you mean, 'supposed to?' Where in the rulebook of life does it say that the sink has to be scoured *every time* you do the dinner dishes?"

I told him I was raised that it is what you're supposed to do every evening.

Rick fired back in frustration as he felt like he had just gotten in trouble, "Well, good for you. How was I supposed to know that? I was not raised to scour the sink every time I cleaned the kitchen. If you want to do that, knock yourself out."

This was the beginning of us encountering many *unspoken rules* that we had not identified as such.

Like all newlyweds, we were getting to know one another on an intimate level, and not just sexually but practically as we were now living with each other. For the better part of our first year of dating and right up to our wedding, we never argued. We always seemed to agree on just about everything; our relationship was fun, vibrant, and alive.

However, after we got married, things started to change. We began quarreling about the dumbest things, mostly because we didn't know how each of us was wired and therefore did not know how to effectively communicate with one another.

One evening, after Rick loaded the dishwasher—not even five minutes later, I began rearranging the dishes inside of it.

Rick was a little annoyed and asked, "What are you doing? I already loaded it."

"I know, but you did it wrong."

Defensively he responded, "Wrong, how did I load it 'wrong?' Did I try to cram the cups where the silverware goes? Did I put the plates where the cups went and vice versa?"

"No, not that. You loaded the glasses from the front to the back. You're supposed to load them from the back to the front."

Rick busted out in laughter, "Are you kidding me? Where did you come up with that? Maybe I should just let you do the dinner dishes so the dishwasher gets loaded the way you want and the sink gets scoured every evening. Apparently, your way is the best way."

The two of us were irritated with each other for the rest of that evening.

If the constant arguing between us was not enough as we were learning to live with one another, I also felt that Rick didn't care about my safety. At bedtime every night, he brushed his

CHAPTER 3: A NEW BEGINNING

teeth and jumped right into bed. I'd ask if he had checked the sliding glass door and windows and locked the front door. Rick typically said he was sure all was okay, but he never actually went to check. So, I went around and did what I'd always seen my father do at night. Unbeknownst to me, his response was merely stemming from the fact that his family never locked up at night the way my family did. It was not even on Rick's radar to do so. Unfortunately, this began a small feeling inside that made me feel not valued or loved. This feeling grew over the years as Rick continued the habit of not locking up our home.

A few months went by, and we were starting to get into the groove of living with one another. Grasping how to communicate effectively with each other was a struggle we battled for years to come. Both of us being firstborns, strong-willed, and sarcastic didn't help either.

I began to get homesick and missed being around my family who lived more than a thousand miles north of us. When Rick came home from work one evening, I asked him if he would be okay moving to the Pacific Northwest.

Rick didn't hesitate and said he was all for the adventure since he had lived in Southern California his whole life. The two of us made arrangements to end our current employment, and we made the trek up north. Shortly after getting to Olympia, Rick found work at a local concrete block manufacturing company. He hated that job because it had nothing to do with his calling to be a pastor. However, he needed to provide for our financial needs, so he took the work the Lord had given him.

RICK: A couple months went by, and I came home from a hard day's work to the new one-bedroom apartment we had moved

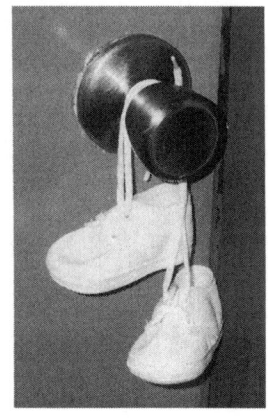

into. As I made my way up the stairwell to the front door, I noticed something strange dangling from the exterior doorknob of our apartment. There they were: cute little white newborn baby shoes. I froze. I didn't move and just stared at the shoes, realizing what Tiffany's message was to me.

I opened the door slowly and came around the corner to see her sitting on the couch smiling, and I said with a shocked look on my face, "SHUT UP! Are you serious?" She nodded yes and laughed. The two of us hugged, as we both came to grips that we were going to be parents.

Nine months later on April 1, Kaleb Michael Peter Bulman was born. He was 9 pounds, 5 ounces, 22 inches long and healthy. Tiffany did great! I was so proud of her. We sobbed like babies as we together held our gift from God right there in the delivery room.

As expected, a new baby tested the resolve of our relationship. Not only were we learning to function as a married couple, we also had a baby boy added to the mix. I loved Tiffany and Kaleb more than life itself. However, many years later, I realized my actions—or lack thereof—seemed to communicate differently to Tiffany.

TIFFANY: Some time went by, and one evening I came home from the grocery store and had only a couple of bags in my hand. Rick asked if he could help, but I told him no since I just had the two sacks in my hand.

A few days later, I did a big grocery run. When I came home, before unloading the car, I brought Kaleb into our apartment—

CHAPTER 3: A NEW BEGINNING

our *second-floor* apartment. I was hoping Rick would run downstairs and begin unloading the groceries from the car while I stayed with our son and put the groceries away. NOT SO MUCH.

Rick immediately grabbed Kaleb, sat back on the couch, and started to play with him. There I was, left to begin the million and one trips from the car to the apartment. Frustrated after what felt like my 18th trip I sarcastically said, "You just sit there; I've got it all!"

Rick, who I loved (and still do dearly) could be clueless in his younger years. I couldn't believe he asked, "What are you talking about?" He added, "I figured if you needed help you would have just asked."

I was blown away by his response. I could feel my anger rising and snapped back at him, "Why should I have to ask? Why can't you just offer to help every time? Or, just do it for me?"

He seemed to blow me off with, "Whatever."

As I put the groceries away, I was baffled by his unwillingness just to help. I began thinking maybe he just didn't care about me. He was not doing certain things that communicated that he loved me.

RICK: My laziness, which Tiffany perceived as of lack of caring for her went on for months. Sadly, I allowed her to do everything—the cleaning, the cooking, caring for Kaleb, changing light bulbs in the apartment, fixing doorknobs, and doing the laundry. Every night, she cleaned the kitchen after dinner and then made my lunch for the following day.

I had this mentality that because I worked 50 to 60 hours a week at a very labor-intensive job, I needed to just rest in the evenings and weekends to recuperate. I figured, and I'm genuinely embarrassed to say, because Tiffany was a stay-at-home mom, the apartment was her domain. I had a lot to learn. I was clueless and causing damage to our relationship.

Unfortunately, things did not change for us. I kept working and leaving everything up to Tiffany. One evening as she cleaned a broiler pan, I heard what sounded like a gun going off over and over and over again. There was a constant banging that was deafening. I rushed into the kitchen to see her slamming the metal broiler pan into the tin sink repeatedly.

I yelled to be heard over the loud crash being made with the pan against the tin sink, "Hey! Hey! Hey! What in the heck are you doing?!"

Tiffany looked at me and said, "I can't get this freaking pan clean!"

"Are you kidding me right now?" I asked in disbelief. Self-righteously I added, "One, you're scaring Kaleb with all this racket. Two, you're scaring me; this is weird behavior; it's only a pan. And, three, you can't typically clean a broiler pan spotless anyway." Tiffany put the pan and SOS pad down, left the kitchen, and took Kaleb. The two of them went into the bedroom for her to cool off.

Unbeknownst to me *at the time*, Tiffany was snapping and caving under the pressure because of the lack of help she got from me. Her issue was not that the broiler pan was hard to clean; the problem was I was not helping out like I should have been, which brought her to a breaking point.

TIFFANY: The next day, I went to my parent's house while Rick was at work. I began to vent to my mom, "I don't understand. Rick just comes home after work, eats his dinner, and sits on the couch. He doesn't help with anything. He doesn't clean up the

CHAPTER 3: A NEW BEGINNING

kitchen after dinner or help clean in general, and he doesn't offer to help with Kaleb. I always have to ask. For crying out loud, he doesn't even make his lunch for the next day. I do it all!" I remember crying; I was beyond frustrated.

My mom replied empathetically, "Honey, he needs to realize he can't leave everything to you, especially now that Kaleb is here. You need to have a conversation with him and see what he's thinking."

That evening I approached Rick to talk. I told him I needed more of his help when he was home and that I could not keep doing everything. He had an interesting response that seemed to shed some light on his lack of helping out.

He said, "You told me I didn't need to help you clean at the end of the day. You said it was something you simply enjoyed doing and you didn't expect me to help. Remember when we had that conversation right after we got married?"

Admittedly, I did remember telling him that, and it did explain his lack of action, but I was a little surprised that he took my statement as a *lifelong* rule. "That was over two years ago, and now we have a child. I need to take that statement back. I need your help. It's too much for one person."

Rick seemed to understand where I was coming from and promised to help out more. I was relieved that he agreed to be of more help, but I did notice how he still was not taking on the responsibility of locking up the apartment at night. I was not able to identify why just yet, but that hurt me. I could not figure out why he did not value our family enough to make sure we were all safely locked inside for the evening.

As time went on, Rick did put some effort into helping me. He started cleaning the kitchen after dinner, which naturally led him to make his lunch, while I bathed Kaleb. All of which did help and provided a little relief for me.

HEART CHECK

Love is patient, love is kind. It does not envy, it does not boast, it is not proud. It does not dishonor others, it is not self-seeking, it is not easily angered, it keeps no record of wrongs. Love does not delight in evil but rejoices with the truth.

I CORINTHIANS 13:4–6

// 1. What did you love about your spouse when you first met and began dating?

_____
_____
_____
_____
_____
_____
_____

Have you forgotten about those qualities?

_____
_____
_____
_____

Do those qualities still *bless* you or *bother* you?

_____
_____
_____
_____

// 2. What unspoken rules have you encountered in your relationship?

_____
_____
_____
_____
_____
_____
_____

// 3. List ways you have resolved your relational issues because of unspoken rules.

_____
_____
_____
_____
_____
_____

// 4. What are ways you love and cherish your spouse?

// 5. How do you currently meet the emotional needs of your spouse?

CHAPTER 4

DING! FIGHTING IN THIS CORNER
NOT A FAIRY-TALE REALITY

RICK: Over the years, our family grew. We welcomed the birth of two more sons, Joshua and Jared, and eventually, our daughter, Faith. We were a church-going family who loved Jesus and were heavily involved in volunteer ministry. I served as a children's worker, youth pastor, associate pastor, and everything in between. Tiffany led worship and was part of every children's ministry at the churches we attended during that time.

On the outside, we looked great. Perceived by many to be a happy family who genuinely had a heart for people. However, like most couples with kids, what was seen on the outside was a different reality than what was taking place behind closed doors. Yes, there were a lot of great days and seasons, but the not-so-great days and seasons were dark, combative, and out of control at times.

I did improve in helping Tiffany here and there, as well as with the kids. However, I will admit, I still slipped into a self-centered mode when visiting family or at church or a gathering of some kind. It was in these moments and environments that I forgot to help out or even ask Tiffany if she needed help. I was always focused on the people I was interacting with and not Tiffany and the kids. Unaware of my immaturity at the time, this type of behavior was the reason for a lot of conflict between us.

Tiffany got frustrated trying to corral all four kids when we were at church or a get-together. Sometimes she had to hunt me down to help her. When she eventually found me, she'd approach me in a fast-paced manner, aggravated and typically with a child in tow. Feeling like a single parent, she'd thrust the child she was having an issue with into my arms. She often said, "Please take (name of offending child)! I'm done!" And then she immediately turned around and walked off.

Embarrassed and noticing the awkward look on the person's face I was talking with, I'd laugh it off and make light of it, saying something like, "Oh-oh, momma isn't happy. Isn't raising kids peaceful and easy? NOT!" Typically, the other person took my cue and politely chuckled along.

Later I'd tell Tiffany how the incident embarrassed me and made the individual I was with feel uncomfortable. Tiffany said that embarrassing me was not her intent and she'd apologize.

However, she did go on to say, "I'm also not a single parent of four kids. I need you to be more present when we're out and not just at home. I was having a difficult time with (name of offending child) and you were nowhere to be found. When I finally did find you, I was frustrated. But, again, I'm sorry."

I told her I understood where she was coming from and, of course, forgave her. However, my actions in the future did not prove to Tiffany that I understood because I did not change.

These public encounters with Tiffany continued to happen through the years, and they seemed to intensify. Her moments of irritation with our children often caused me to reflect on when she had "lost it" over cleaning the broiler pan. I assigned the

CHAPTER 4: DING! FIGHTING IN THIS CORNER

responsibility of her anger solely to her—as if she was not justified for being upset. I was clueless that my behavior might be the spark that lit the fuse that set Tiffany off. I was blind to the reality that I was exasperating her by neglecting my husbandly duties.

Tiffany's irritation with me grew exponentially. I could see it in her responses toward me and at times, with our children. However, I viewed the intensity of her anger as a lack of self-control, which it may have been. But because I viewed it that way, I dismissed it as non-warranted emotion. Yes, she could have controlled her feelings better when out in public or privately at home, but my distorted view fueled impatience with Tiffany in this area of our marriage, and it would set her off.

My politeness started to become more direct, sometimes using abusive words. What started out as polite requests to not behave angrily became very demeaning and abusive statements:

A few years of: "Can you please not do that?"

Then, a couple of years of: "I've asked you not to do this many times. What's going on?"

Then, a few years of: "Hello, what's your problem? I'm tired of asking you to stop!"

Then, around year seven, it transitioned into: "There's something wrong with you! You need help!"

Then, around year 10 it was no holds barred: "You're crazy! You're not right in the head! Are you possessed?"

My inability to control my mouth, regardless of Tiffany's words or actions, was damaging her. I was abusing her with my words and tearing down her spirit. She was aware of her anger, but being told she was psycho and out of control was not helping. It only made her feel worse about herself.

This caused the *fight or flight* side of Tiffany to kick in. Often her strong-willed nature came out, and it was an all-out war between us. This type of verbal abuse was tearing her down so much emotionally that she began to lose respect for me.

I wish I would have had the wisdom of Jewish Rabbi Abraham Joshua Heschel when he said, "Words create worlds."[4] I was naïve to the reality that words are more tangible than we think—they actually stick to people. That is what I did with Tiffany. I created a world where she was torn down emotionally and made to believe something she was not—that she was crazy. She already suspected my love for her was not deep due to my lack of caring for the household. My tearing her down verbally only made things worse.

This abuse coupled with me not making sure she and the kids were safe at night by locking them in, not taking care of the cars, and not responding to her requests for me to do yard work or fix things made her naturally edgy toward me.

TIFFANY: One day while I was cleaning up after lunch, we started to argue. Rick seemed more preoccupied with work than he was with fixing some things I had asked him to repair.

"You care more about your work than you do our family!"

"Are you kidding me? I work hard for our family."

I went on to make my case with my back turned to Rick as I washed the silverware in the kitchen sink, "I ask you to do things repeatedly, and you don't do them. I've been asking for six months for you to rehang the broken towel rack in the bathroom!"

"I told you I'd get to it—"

I interrupted him and said sarcastically, "Yeah, but I want it done in this lifetime. Do you think you can manage to get it done before the kids graduate from college?" I know my attitude and

---

4. Heschel, A.J. (1996). *Moral Grandeur and Spiritual Audacity*. New York, NY: Farrar, Straus, and Giroux Publishing Company. viii.

CHAPTER 4: DING! FIGHTING IN THIS CORNER

snippiness was not helping—my irritation was getting the better of me at that moment.

Rick responded in a way that instantly fueled my anger. "Look, I have a *real* job that requires me to work 40 to 50 hours a week. You *just* stay at home wiping butts and noses all day. If you want it done so badly, you can do it!"

TIME OUT! We laugh about this incident now. When we share what happened next, Rick often says that if he could travel back in time to 27-year-old Rick, he'd smack him and put him in a chokehold until he took back that stupid, idiotic, naïve statement and beg for forgiveness from me for even thinking something so asinine.

TIME IN! Without thinking, I turned around and threw what I had in my hand (a table knife) at him. Yikes! The knife landed literally between his feet and stuck in the kitchen's linoleum floor with the handle upward. In shock, he looked at me. I glared at him with one eyebrow raised, pretending as if I'd meant to do that, but I was surprised as well.

"You're insane!" Rick yelled. "You're out of control!"

Over the next day or so, we made up. In fact, I apologized and told Rick I was sorry for throwing the knife at him and had not realized what I had in my hand at that moment. For all I knew, it could have been a spoon.

"I know," he chuckled. "You're not talented enough to accurately throw a knife and have it land by sticking perfectly between my feet. Although, it was impressive." We laughed, hugged, and decided to move on from there.

Both of us have lost our temper with each other, which has resulted in regrettable actions. One day Rick got very mad because he realized he was wrong about something, but he did not want to admit it.

While I was sitting at the dining room table eating soup, he flipped my bowl causing a ridiculous mess and loud noise as the porcelain bowl came back down violently on the glass tabletop. Soup went everywhere. It was on the wall, floor, kitchen window, and, yes, even on me. He left the house quickly. He told me later he knew he had messed up big time. These regrettable moments were damaging to our relationship.

Unfortunately, things did not get better between us. Rick's disrespect and verbal abuse when I got mad was destroying me and driving a wedge in our relationship. We were caught in a vicious cycle that we were unable to get out of on our own.

RICK: The first time things came to a head between us was at Christmas when we went to my sister's house to spend the holiday with my side of the family. Tiffany was already anticipating being left to take care of our kids while I sat around enjoying my family. This well-deserved anticipation, based on previous experiences, made her blood simmer before we even arrived.

Two days into the visit, around 8 p.m. on Christmas Day, Tiffany's concern about me abandoning her with our kids had come true. She had put Kaleb and Joshua to bed. For two hours Kaleb kept goofing off and messing with Joshua. Josh would start to cry, causing Tiffany to go into the room and try to regain order and get the two of them to sleep.

In the meantime, I just sat there on the couch visiting with family. Finally, Tiffany snapped at me. Every head turned, and immediate silence took over the room. I was embarrassed. "Umm, what's going on?" I said. Stupid question because I should have realized Tiffany had been going back and forth into the room for the last two hours trying to get the boys to go to sleep.

CHAPTER 4: DING! FIGHTING IN THIS CORNER

Suddenly, she grabbed Kaleb by the arm and ushered him into another bedroom. I finally caught a clue and jumped right up and followed them. It seemed as if Kaleb was about to get the spanking of a lifetime. Our rule was that we would never spank in anger. By default, in this situation, I needed to be the one issuing the spanking (if warranted). I got in between Tiffany and Kaleb and asked her what happened.

She unloaded on me, "I've been trying to get the boys asleep for two hours, and every time I get Joshua asleep, Kaleb wakes him back up. I have given him plenty of warnings; now, he is getting punished!"

Still standing between the two of them, I said, "Honey, calm down and let me handle it."

"Calm down!" she snapped at me. "Oh, now you want to help? You don't get to sit on your butt all weekend long and then swoop in and try to be the hero and take over parenting. Move and give me Kaleb!"

"No! You're too angry. I will handle this."

Tiffany aggressively came at Kaleb, but I said, "STOP! You're not going to touch him!"

This only infuriated her. She reached for him, but I stuck both arms out to stop her. What I meant to be a light push just to keep her from coming to get Kaleb, turned into her stepping backward onto a stack of folded-down Macy's gift boxes. Because they were stacked on top of one another, the stack was very slippery. Tiffany's back foot slid out from underneath her causing her to fall. I immediately felt awful because I had not meant for her to fall; I just wanted her to step back and not get to Kaleb.

Reaching to help her up, I said, "Oh honey! I'm sorry. You stepped on the Macy's boxes and you slipped. I didn't mean for you to fall. Are you okay?"

"Get away from me!" she yelled.

At that moment, there was a knock on the bedroom door. It was my mom wanting to make sure everything was okay. She took Kaleb and left us to sort things out. Tiffany wanted to go home immediately and started to pack up the room we were all staying in.

I was distraught and called our pastor; I did not know what to do. He told me we could meet the next day to chat. We loaded up our minivan and drove the two and half hours back home that Christmas night. It was horrible.

The next morning I heard a knock on the front door. It was Pastor Brian and our mutual friend, Jim. "Rick, get your shoes on. We're going for a hike!" Pastor Brian announced. Our home was at the base of a mountain, which made for nice long walks. The three of us headed out and up the mountain.

As we walked, I shared the trouble we were having along with everything that had happened the night before. "Tiffany accused me of not helping out, and when I do offer to help, she gets mad at me," I explained.

Obviously, there are always two sides to every story. Pastor Brian and Jim knew this, of course, having many more years of married life under their belts. They began to probe and ask questions, which revealed the full story. They explained to me that not helping Tiffany and leaving everything up to her had pushed her to the edge.

I began to see that had I been helping the entire time during our visit, she might not have gotten to her breaking point. Although we acknowledged that her behavior was not warranted, if I loved my wife as Christ loved the church (Ephesians 5:25), I would have been serving her the entire time, making the visit pleasant for everyone.

CHAPTER 4: DING! FIGHTING IN THIS CORNER

Pastor Brian asked me if he could be honest about things he had observed between Tiffany and me.

"Of course."

"You do not love your wife well. I've witnessed on more than one occasion you making things difficult for her."

I wondered what he meant by that.

He continued, "You don't serve her the way Jesus calls husbands to care for their wives. Your willingness to not tend to her needs promptly, the lack of consideration you have for her, and your—to be honest—laziness in helping with your kids are wrong and weighing on your wife. That is why she may be a bit edgy."

"Wait a minute. What do you mean by my 'lack of consideration?'" I was clueless.

"On three separate occasions I've witnessed you in a corporate gathering get up to get coffee, more food, or a dessert of some kind, *never* stopping to think to ask Tiffany if she wanted something while you were up."

I naïvely tried to defend myself with the lame answer of, "Well, I figured if she wanted something she'd ask me or just get it herself."

Jim laughed out loud in disbelief and said, "If your mentality doesn't change, you're not only going to have a very long and hard road ahead of you, but you will run the risk of pushing your wife away and potentially lose her." (Jim spoke from experience since he was on his second marriage, but this time, the marriage was going well because Jesus was at the center of it.)

For the first time, I started to see that maybe the problem was not just Tiffany. Perhaps I was contributing negatively in ways I was not aware.

That day, Pastor Brian and Jim continued to coach and encourage me. They revealed their failures in their own marriages.

They both owned up to various shortcomings between them and their wives that had caused intense arguments. They wanted to let me know we were not alone nor the only couple to go through such hardships.

I thanked them for their time, and I tried to listen and heed to their advice.

Things improved significantly for a while. I'd have moments of greatness and then not so much. I was getting better at accomplishing Tiffany's to-do lists promptly. I was putting effort into asking her if she needed help before waiting for her to ask for it, and I started offering her coffee when I went to get some.

Then, something incredible started to happen. The more my attitude and actions began to align with God's way of how husbands should serve their wives, peace began to reside in our home. I noticed that the more I helped Tiffany, the more she reciprocated. For the first time in years, we started experiencing the love and attraction we had when we were dating.

BUT! Sadly it only lasted a couple of years. *SIGH!*

HEART CHECK

Get rid of all bitterness, rage, anger, harsh words, and slander, as well as all types of evil behavior. Instead, be kind to each other, tenderhearted, forgiving one another, just as God through Christ has forgiven you.
EPHESIANS 4:31–32 (NLT)

// 1. Describe what *great* days look like in your relationship.

_____
_____
_____
_____
_____

// 2. Describe what your *not-so-great* days (seasons) look like in your relationship.

_____
_____
_____
_____
_____

// **3. How is your *outside* (visible) relationship different from your *inside* (at home) relationship?**

_____
_____
_____
_____
_____
_____

// **4. List hindrances, roadblocks, or unspoken rules that impede unity in your relationship.**

_____
_____
_____
_____
_____
_____

How do you deal with these hindrances, roadblocks, or unspoken rules?

_____
_____
_____
_____
_____
_____

Do you work at removing them or have you become accustomed to them, and therefore accept it will always be a fighting match?

// 5. **What steps could you take to remove those hindrances, roadblocks, or unspoken rules?**

CHAPTER 5

RICK'S MISTRESS
WORK, WIFE, AND LIFE

---//---

RICK: For the first ten years of our marriage, we mostly lived paycheck to paycheck. The Lord always provided, but finances were tight as we raised our four children. I was working for a water company that provided bottled water service; I had a route in Seattle. It was a good job and allowed me to be home in the evenings and on weekends.

One day I was on the phone with my friend, John, who had been the best man at our wedding. He had started a mortgage company in Chino, California, and shared his experience in launching his new venture. He went on to explain that he had people cold-calling residents from leads he received from title companies: at that time, FHA was issuing refunds to homeowners and one of the ways to get that refund was by refinancing their mortgage.

Because interest rates were dropping, people wanted to do it. I jokingly told John that if he ever wanted to break into the Pacific Northwest market to let me know and I would cold-call for him. He told me to talk it over with Tiffany, and if we were comfortable with the idea, he would install a phone line in our home and I could get started. Tiffany and I decided to give this a try, but only working 7:00–9:00 p.m. on Tuesdays and Thursdays. I acquired some leads to call and away I went.

Sitting on a milk crate and utilizing a folding card table as a desk, I began calling in our garage. Much to my surprise, I was pretty good at it. Within the two-hour timeframe we had agreed to, I was getting a minimum of two or three applications each night.

John was impressed. I was producing more applications for refinances during my four hours of work each week than some of his full-time employees. These leads turned into loans and those loans, once funded, would pay me a small commission. Within a three-month period, I was making five times what I made delivering water. After prayerful consideration, Tiffany and I agreed that we should step out in faith and have me quit delivering water and pursue launching a satellite office for John's company in our town.

John flew in from California, and he and I scouted locations. Once we found the right office space, we signed a lease, bought furniture, and I began my new career!

Within the first three months, I was achieving the success we had hoped for. I learned the business beyond cold-calling. I was closing loans and immediately became one of John's top producers. Tiffany and I were blown away by what felt like a windfall of income that came our way. With *integrity*, I was helping people with their mortgages and placing them in a better financial situation. It was fulfilling and lucrative.

For the first time in our ten-year marriage, money was not an issue as I began pushing six figures. However, my competitive nature started to get the best of me and *almost* attaining a six-figure income was not enough, I had to get there.

I began working harder and more extended hours. I hired a couple more employees and started networking with other loan

CHAPTER 5: RICK'S MISTRESS

officers, which tripled my workload; making six figures became attainable and then some. This success drove me to work harder and longer. I brought my work home with me. Clients and/or my employees called my cell phone after hours, all needing advice. I felt I always had to take the call because it meant more business. It, unfortunately, became commonplace for me to get up from eating dinner with my family while saying, "Honey, I have to take this call; it's a new loan!" Tiffany often thought, "You always have to take the call."

TIFFANY: I was incredibly grateful for Rick's commitment and his work ethic, and the income was terrific. However, I began to despise his cell phone. I quickly started to feel I was in second place after his job. It was if his career was his *mistress*. I felt like the children and I were only good for his leftover time; it seemed he loved his work more than our family.

Rick had this warped mentality that because he was providing financial freedom for our household, we all should be okay with losing him to his work in the evenings and weekends. We owned a home, as well as new cars, and started taking trips together. However, even while on vacation, Rick still broke away to work from time to time. Again, it made me feel like his first love was not me or our family—his first love was his job.

Because of his success, we were able to sell our first home and build a new one that was twice the size. Life was good, according to Rick. However, life, marriage, and family were not so good for me. I was competing with my husband's job and resented him for it. Even the kids started to feel this way.

A few years into working for John, Rick's office grew from a one-man operation to 30 employees. Things were firing on all cylinders, except our marriage. Our kids complained that he was always on his phone. It was difficult to make excuses for him because I felt the same way. If we couldn't find Rick around the house, it would not be odd for one of the kids to sarcastically say, "He's probably on his cell phone somewhere working."

I remember one day when Rick was out front playing catch with Joshua, who was 12 at the time. Shortly after they started playing, Rick's cell phone rang and he took the call, completely unaware of the sick feeling his behavior had produced in our son.

For the next few minutes, they continued to play catch. Rick caught the football with one hand while holding his *precious* cell phone in the other. Josh finally had enough! He caught his last pass from Rick and then placed the ball on the street and walked away. Rick was shocked and put his client on hold and asked where Josh was going.

With disdain in his voice, Josh said, "You don't want to play catch with me. You just want to work." He left Rick standing in the middle of the street and went inside.

I know what Josh felt like. We were in the car with friends during my birthday party when Rick took a work-related phone call at 10 p.m. I was embarrassed and felt he was getting a call from his number one love, his *mistress*—his job.

RICK: John's company was growing rapidly. He needed a second in command and chose me to be Vice President of Sales. This position came with a hefty six-figure salary and a company car. The two of us traveled to meet in various cities, growing the company by hiring more loan officers. We eventually grew to 100 employees. All the traveling left Tiffany at home fending for herself and the kids; unfortunately, something she was used to

CHAPTER 5: RICK'S MISTRESS

doing. The upside was that the money was good. The downside: it was at the expense of my marriage and children.

John eventually approached me and offered to *double* my salary if we would move down to California. He needed his VP in the office with him. Because of my position and responsibilities, it was becoming too complicated to work remotely. Tiffany hated the idea. She knew in her heart that if we went, even though I wouldn't be traveling as much, she would still feel alone and disregarded. At least living where her friends and family were, Tiffany could face the loneliness by visiting with them. After many fights, I got Tiffany to say yes to the idea, but inside she was digging in her heels.

We made the move, but after four short months in California, I learned that John was selling his company to a local banker. The president of the bank sat in my office and asked me to stay on as a VP of a division within his company. However, there was one issue—he could not pay me the salary I was getting from John. Although his offer was still generous, Tiffany and I felt we were not to accept it. We both sensed God telling us to move back to the Pacific Northwest. Making this decision meant stepping down as a vice president since there was no office to come back to where we had once lived. It meant I would have to start all over gaining new clients and producing loans.

Our home had not sold during the four months we were gone. We took it off the market and moved back into it. Now working remotely from home, I tried to acquire loans and started a consulting business within the local real estate community.

In my new career, I applied the same intensity I had when I opened my office with John. Long days and long nights became a typical work schedule. Tiffany and I argued because she and the kids were not getting an ample amount of my time. I'd say that I had to work harder to get my consulting business off the ground. She honestly felt like I was married to my work. She expressed how she hated competing with my *mistress*. I foolishly believed that once I was successful, she and the kids would understand and end up being okay.

Unfortunately, over the next two years, I was not successful. I had many promising ideas and business, but nothing came to fruition. In short, we ended up losing it all. We could not make our mortgage, car, and credit card payments.

I started to fall into depression. I cried out to God multiple times and heard nothing. I told Tiffany that because we loved Jesus, served in our local church, and were faithful tithers, God wouldn't allow us to lose everything. I believed God wouldn't have us experience such loss because He was a caring and faithful heavenly Father. I did not know God as well as I thought. My theology was way off.

As loving and devoted as God is, my mentality was like I had forgotten about all the verses in the Bible that warned people (Christians too) that they would encounter troubling times (Psalm 23:4; James 1:2; 1 Peter 4:12). Or, I thought I was exempt from having to deal with such hardship. Either way, God *lovingly* and in His infinite wisdom, allowed us to lose it all to realign us to Him. No one needed to realign more than me. I needed to experience some humility to draw me back into a right relationship with the Lord.

I had to get an actual job and stop pursuing anything mortgage-related. The market was different. It had imploded, and the industry was not the same. I went back to the water company where I once worked, but this time I went into the sales department rather than being a route driver.

Making minimum wage plus *a very low* commission while going door-to-door selling bottled water services challenged

CHAPTER 5: RICK'S MISTRESS

my ego. I met my quota each month but was dying a thousand deaths doing this type of work. I often sat in my work van and cried thinking about the position I once had and the money I once made working for John.

Now I was getting apartment doors slammed in my face because people didn't want to be bothered. I was being broken, and this is right where God wanted me. It was my brokenness that brought me to my knees over and over again.

The good news was that during this season, I was not all about my work anymore. I hated my job so much I couldn't wait to get home and just be with my family. As stressful as this time was in our lives, there was a modicum of peace in the home because I wasn't working as much.

I didn't stay at the water company long. A business that I had sold water service to was impressed with my sales ability and offered me a job with a decent salary. It was nothing like the mortgage industry, but it was a modest livable wage for a family of six. Eight months later, that job led me to a more lucrative position with another company.

Life seemed to be mellowing out and getting back on track. However, there was a lot of unknown damage that had taken place during our 17-year marriage. Tiffany and I had relationship issues we had never dealt with. We never got counseling, but instead made the mistake of sweeping the past under the rug and got excited when new blessings and adventures came along.

Just as things got back on track for us financially, I ended up being let go from my job when my company lost their Microsoft account. That account afforded them the ability to staff the people they wanted, and when they lost it, I was one of those employees who got laid off. This time, Tiffany and I did not freak out. We had lost everything and saw how God provided for us once before. We decided to reflect on God's past successes, which produced a present peace that gave us hope for the future.

This was a season of extreme growth for both of us. Over the next eight months, I could not find work. I had an Excel worksheet with more than 400 different jobs I had applied for and was turned down by every one of them. I was even turned down by a pizza delivery company.

This tested my resolve, and yes, there was tension between Tiffany and me. The miracle of it all was that even though I was not working, every bill got paid and our family never starved. We had never experienced such miraculous provision before.

TIFFANY: Rick and I were always heavily involved in our church family. We had seasons of paid and non-paid positions. We always desired to serve in the area of our giftings. Rick always felt called to be a senior pastor, and I believed that mantle was on him. Over the years, even though Rick worked full-time, he was able to maintain his pastoral credentials because of the level of his involvement at our church. The various ministry roles he had been involved in over the years had prepared Rick for what God had next for our family. Ministry was Rick's real passion, and the yearning to be a senior pastor was strong in his heart.

During this off-season, Rick tirelessly networked with district supervisors in our denomination, with the blessing and backing of our pastor and friend, Eric. This led to Rick being offered his first senior pastorate. We were excited to see how the Lord was orchestrating everything leading up to this moment. We began to make logistical plans for our transition to our new assignment.

As much as I saw this as an exciting adventure for Rick and our family, I was gripped with fear at the same time. I often had

CHAPTER 5: RICK'S MISTRESS

haunting thoughts of continuous neglect from my husband. I recall thinking from time to time, "If he put his secular career before the kids and me, what will it be like when he's doing ministry? Will the ministry become his new mistress?"

What made this scary for me was that I already saw him planning and strategizing for his new job—when he should have been spending time with the family. His work behavior was a trigger for me; it felt like he always had a girlfriend on the side who seemed to get most of his attention. I started resenting his new role as senior pastor before it even began.

After 17 years of marriage, Rick did help a bit more, but he still neglected his husbandly duties of caring for the family home. I was always baffled that it was like pulling teeth to get him to fix something, change a light bulb, or clean a dirty vent. He'd work in the yard, but for some reason he felt it was beneath him—or so it seemed.

And, the biggie for me was that he still never locked our family in at night. I had grown accustomed to checking every window and locking every door, frequently asking myself, "Does he really not care about us? Wouldn't a husband want to personally make sure everything was secured and his family was safely locked inside?" These unresolved hurtful issues ran deep in my heart, even deeper than I realized.

At this point in our marriage, I was depleted. The years of verbal abuse I endured when we fought—coupled with the neglect and constant feeling of *not being important*—had put me in a funk. My walk with the Lord was mechanical at best; I felt distant from Him and all alone in a marriage that seemed to do nothing but drain me.

Not only had I found myself disconnected from a real intimate relationship with Jesus, the same was true about my husband. I started medicating by drinking wine. At first, wine was something I occasionally enjoyed with a meal, but the occasional glass turned to two glasses and then three glasses and so on. I found that wine took the edge off, and this started me down the path of using this beverage to cope with the gaping hole in my heart because of the state of my marriage and feeling lost in general.

Just before our move up north, Rick was making plans to start his new ministry position, and the enemy (Satan and his troops) was doing all he could to thwart God's new direction for our family by trying to destroy our marriage. It was as if the enemy himself said, "Now! Unleash hell on them."

HEART CHECK

For where your treasure is, there your heart will be also.
MATTHEW 6:21

// 1. What activities do you give most of your time and energy to?

_____
_____
_____
_____
_____
_____
_____

// 2. Prioritize the five most important things in your life today, starting with the most important to the least important within this list.

1. _____
2. _____
3. _____
4. _____
5. _____

// **3. Ask your spouse if they would agree and have them create *their* list for *you*.**

1. _____
2. _____
3. _____
4. _____
5. _____

// **4. Describe how you are nurturing your relationship with:**

- God: _____
- Spouse: _____
- Children: _____
- Work: _____
- Ministry: _____

// **5. List areas you are currently neglecting?**

_____
_____
_____
_____
_____
_____
_____
_____

CHAPTER 6

THE BETRAYAL
THE ULTIMATE DOUBLE BIND

Note: some names and identifying details have been changed to protect the privacy of individuals.

TIFFANY: It was summertime and about one month before Rick started his new role as senior pastor that we needed to find a temporary place to live. We had to be out of our rental but were not quite ready to make the move up north. A friend of ours generously offered us a temporary residence for our family.

As exciting as this new venture was, it was difficult because we would be moving away from many of our friends, like Chad and Lauren. We had known them for a few years and we got along well.

During this time of transition for us, Lauren and Chad were away volunteering at a youth resource retreat center. They had a one-year-old child who needed someone to help take care of while they were working. Lauren asked me if I could help with her young one, but it would require me to stay overnight at the retreat center. I, along with our daughter Faith, accepted Lauren's invitation.

One evening during the retreat, Chad approached me and asked if we could talk about parenting styles since they had one child and we had four. They were newly married and Rick and I had been married for 17 years up to that point, and were ahead of them regarding family and raising children. I didn't think anything of his invite and gladly accepted.

The two of us sat around a fire chatting. At the end of the conversation, he said, "Thank you so much for your time. I appreciate your advice."

And, as he walked away, he said with a chuckle, "You know, I've always had a crush on you." It was awkward and took me by surprise. I didn't say anything, but simply smiled and naïvely thought he was just trying to be cute in an endearing, funny kind of way.

We both left in opposite directions. However, the comment was flattering. I was completely surprised someone ten years younger than me would say or even think such a thing.

While we were living in our transitional housing over the next few weeks, Chad would come over when Rick happened to be gone. He would make up an excuse, like being near by and just wanted to check-in and see if we needed anything, as he knew the majority of our stuff was in boxes and we were in transition.

One evening while Rick was gone to meet some of his church staff, Chad texted me, "Hey, I'm close by and I need to kill some time; what are you all doing?"

"Just watching a movie."

He asked if he could come over. Without thinking, I said he could, which was a mistake on my part.

Another evening, he stopped by when Rick happened to be gone, claiming he noticed something in our house that needed work and he wanted to check on it. As Chad had gotten to know us, he realized that Rick hated fixing things. He knew it was not a strength of his—and more importantly, he somehow picked up on it being a sore spot for me.

CHAPTER 6: THE BETRAYAL

One evening, I had just poured a glass of wine and there was a knock on the door, and there he was, again. He stopped by to drop something off. He noticed my glass of wine and asked if he could have some.

"Sure, Rick hates wine. He won't drink it."

"Seriously, I like it. I'll drink with you," he said with a laugh.

At one point, we were alone sitting on the couch (not next to each other), and he asked, "Does Rick ever massage your feet?"

I laughed. "No, he hates feet."

Before I knew it, he grabbed my foot and starting massaging it while saying, "Really? I'll massage your feet."

I was in shock while at the same time flattered by the attention. I can't explain the emotions I had. I was caught off guard and immediately confused. I knew it was wrong, but the feelings that churned inside me filled a gaping emotional hole I didn't realize was present.

Just moments after he grabbed my foot, one of the kids suddenly came back into the living room. Chad chuckled as he let go of my foot. The seed of an emotional affair was planted firmly in my heart. I felt stuck, but sadly allowed the unfamiliar feelings of being looked after linger instead of rebuking them as another man—not my husband—was generating them.

RICK: We finally made our move to start serving the people in our church. I loved it and felt like I was in my wheelhouse. Tiffany was on the worship team and worked in the children's ministry. For the next few months, I slipped back into working long office hours, as well as being guilty of bringing my work home.

Tiffany immediately felt like the church was my *mistress*. That feeling stirred the already deep wound of rejection and being replaced that she had felt for the better part of our marriage. During this time, Chad and Lauren would come and visit us, often staying the night. Tiffany shared her frustration about my long hours with Lauren, along with the constant neglect of me not doing anything around the house.

Chad picked up on her frustration; it seems he saw it as an opportunity to swoop in and seduce my wife. When they came to visit, and I had not come home from the church after working all day, Chad looked for things to fix around my house. He often said, when Lauren was not present, "When was the last time Rick changed the vent in the ceiling?" or "How long has that light bulb been burnt out?" Whenever he made such a comment, he would add, "If I were your husband, I'd do these things for you."

Tiffany felt relief that someone was taking care of her even though it wasn't me. One day, I came home and noticed the front yard had been mowed. I asked if one of our boys had done it.

"No, I did it. I was bored and thought I'd help you out," Chad said. I thought he was just being a friend, but I could not have been more wrong. This went on for almost a year, me being undermined by another man, and Tiffany was falling for his tactics.

TIFFANY: One evening everyone was going to bed upstairs except Chad. He slept downstairs since the room Lauren was in only had a twin bed. I went to the kitchen to get bottled water from the pantry. I stopped at the bottom of the stairs before heading up because he had asked me a question.

Before I knew it, Chad leaned in and kissed me. I was stunned! I didn't know what to do, but quickly pulled back and said, "Umm, okay, umm, ahh, gggoodnight," and then quickly went

CHAPTER 6: THE BETRAYAL

upstairs to our room where Rick was. I felt guilty for multiple reasons, but the sinful carnal side of me felt the ultimate flattery.

Feeling trapped, I felt I couldn't mention it to anyone because of the embarrassment and the line that was crossed. I thought to myself, "Why didn't I smack him?" "Why didn't I pull back quicker?" "Did I lean in and pause as well?" My mind was racing and my heart was pounding as I realized what had happened.

The next day, it was hard to look at Chad, let alone Lauren and *my* husband. I made the mistake of keeping our secret.

Sadly as time went on, these encounters continued and progressed. With great sorrow, grief, and utter regret, over the next three years, Chad and I developed an ongoing affair with zero boundaries.

I had not only stepped over the line but had ventured way beyond it and was living in sin. It felt like the Lord was gone, even though He was present. My relationship with Rick felt destroyed. My drinking at the end of the day was out of hand. I enjoyed wine, but as I had walked away from the Lord and my marriage, I used it to numb the pain of my guilt and shame.

This coping mechanism did drown my remorse; I was fully aware of my actions. However, the drinking had also caused me to be angrier with Rick. Wine not only suppressed my guilt but also exacerbated the tension present between us. I became even more volatile toward him.

RICK: On December 26, 2013, around 2:00 p.m., I was at the church checking on things. While I walked around on the premises, I thought about what the next year had in store for the church and me as the pastor. I tweeted, "The day after & I'm ready to move forward. Praying 2014 makes me more like

 **Rick Bulman** 🔒 @Rbulman2 - 26 Dec 2013
The day after & I'm ready to move forward. Praying 2014 makes me more like Christ. Oops… But w/out the trials. #dontknowhowthatspossible

Christ. Oops… But w/out the trials. #dontknowthatspossible." I had no clue about the bomb that was going to be dropped on our family in eight hours.

At 10:02 p.m. that evening, Lauren saw a text on Chad's iPad that was from Tiffany. She called Tiffany immediately and let her have it. Tiffany played dumb and hung up on Lauren. I asked what the phone call was all about. Immediately, my phone rang, and it was Lauren. She frantically told me about the texts between Tiffany and Chad. While freaking out on the inside, I asked for screenshots, hoping it wasn't true.

I looked at my wife and said, "I'm about to get some screenshots that show you and Chad having an affair. Do you want to come clean or do you want to see the texts first?"

The look on Tiffany's face told me everything I needed to know. With the feeling of being kicked in the stomach, I asked if they had been with each other, other than an emotional affair.

Tiffany slowly nodded, "Yes."

I felt like I was being sucked into a vortex. I could not think and process what she had just admitted. My emotions were racing faster than my brain could handle this horrific news.

"What in the hell were you thinking? Are you kidding me?" I went on to say some choice words that are not worthy of writing. I felt sick to my stomach. I thought I was going to vomit as I experienced the betrayal of a lifetime.

CHAPTER 6: THE BETRAYAL

Not only was I experiencing a deep dark grief in my sudden state of despondency, I was also filled with rage toward Chad. I immediately reached a level of hatred and anger I did not realize I could muster toward another human being. I warred inside between my craving to hurt him in a way that would change his life forever and letting God deal with him while I focused on the well-being of my kids. At that moment, Tiffany was a distant second, an afterthought. I was in no state of mind to process her actions and what she was putting our family through.

I immediately ran outside and called my pastor and friend, Eric. I vented and shared what I had just found out. Stunned and speechless, he empathized with me, trying to ease my pain. He invited me to stay at his house for the evening, which I accepted.

Before I left, I needed to connect with our 17-year-old son, Joshua. He was the only child home that fateful evening. He learned of his mom's affair at the same time I did. Josh was livid with Tiffany, and he did not have a problem letting her know it. His finding out about the affair at the same time I did meant it was a tragic night for him as well. I had to step up to the plate and confront my wife and deal with my emotions, while at the same time, console our son.

Josh was yelling at me in his room, "How could she have done this to you and our family? What was she thinking? What's going to happen now?" Like a machine gun, one after another, he kept firing questions, not giving me a chance to answer. He ended his bombardment of emotion by asking, "How could Chad have done this; he was our friend?"

That triggered a knee-jerk response and without thinking I fired back, "I don't know, but I want to kill him!"

Joshua, not realizing that was simply an emotional statement that was not backed with real intent, looked at me and with eyes wide opened he pleaded, "Please Dad, no! Please don't do anything. Please, I beg you!"

The fear in his eyes that I would actually do something to Chad shook me to my core. I responded, "Buddy, that was just an expression. I promise you that I will not do anything that will make our family's situation worse. Hurting Chad would not serve our family well, because I'd be in jail. You and your brothers and sister are priority number one. Okay?"

With a great sigh of relief, he shook his head yes. But he then asked, "What about Mom?"

All his questions were fair. In my head, I prayed, "God how do I help Josh right now when I have just heard the most crushing news of my life?" The Lord immediately whispered to my heart, "Just speak to what you know is true about Me and *not* what you are currently feeling."

I sat Josh down as I pulled up a chair. The presence of God anointed what was about to come out of my mouth.

"Buddy, this sucks plain and simple. I don't know the answers to your questions, but I'm glad you asked. To be honest, I don't know what's going to happen next for all of us. With that said, let me speak to what I do know. I *know* this is not God's fault. I *know* we all have a free will because God gave man a powerful gift, the gift of choice. Your mom made hers, and we're going to find out why, shortly. What I do *know* is that God is still good and He's still on the throne. I *know* He is our only hope and will be our only true source of strength. I *know* that God is all-powerful and can turn anything around."

Speaking these truths as a wrecked and broken man, I wanted for Josh and me to do what the Apostle Paul instructed in Philippians 4:8, which was to think about whatever things were true, noble, just, pure, and praiseworthy.

CHAPTER 6: THE BETRAYAL

As I attempted to align our hearts and minds with the truth of God's Word and His character, a sense of peace filled the room. Josh begin to calm down and shake his head in agreement with what I was telling him, and then we prayed together. It was the grace of God that gave me the strength to be strong and think clearly while dealing with extreme heartache.

Emotionally distraught, I packed a few things and left Tiffany and Josh at home. I had a two-hour drive to get to Eric's house. On my way, I phoned Dan Driscoll, my best friend. We were childhood friends who knew everything about each other; we're like family.

My phone call woke him up, so I immediately cut to the chase: "Dude, Tiffany has been cheating on me for three years!" Dan was shocked and immediately filled with sadness. Full of anger, rage, and tears flowing down my face, I explained over the phone all I knew about what went on between Tiffany and Chad. In the midst of saying, "Why, why, why! Why, would Tiffany do this to our family and me? What was she thinking? How could this have happened? Why didn't God stop this?" I was trying to figure out how I did not know this was going on.

For the last few years, I knew the relationship between Tiffany and me seemed a little more volatile or strained than normal, but it seemed to me to be typical *married seasonal stress*. I had moved our family and started a new job. I genuinely believed the tension would smooth out soon. Because sex was still great and frequent, and we still had times of laughter together, I truly felt blindsided by this news. Looking back, a major part of my naïveté was that I had my head so deeply buried in my work that I probably was missing a lot of the telltale signs that were right in front of my face. My confusion and turmoil caused me to be a bumbling mess on the phone.

Dan just kindly listened and tried to console me. Being a pastor I knew the statement I was about to make was not theologically correct, but it was what I felt at that moment, "This is big. It's huge! It's so big of a problem, I don't even think God can fix it!"

I remember hearing Dan trying to say something, but it was drowned out by an immediate thought that cut through all emotion and human logic. The response I heard to my accusation about God's inability to fix my problem was: "I can when I have willing hearts."

At that moment, I was convinced the thought came straight from the Holy Spirit. It was so profound to me. With the emotion of rage and hurt present in my heart, peace flooded my soul. The idea that a willing heart offered by Tiffany and me could allow healing and restoration to take place. However, I said to myself, "But I don't know that I'm willing."

Dan stayed on the phone with me as I made my way to my pastor's home. I could not shake the statement I had just heard in my spirit. It was a challenge and sign of hope at the same time. I finally made it to where I was going to stay for the evening; Eric and I talked for a couple of hours before we both called it a night.

That night, when I was alone in the room Eric prepared for me to sleep in, I laid there with my thoughts racing. I thought about what Tiffany did, how this might affect our family, and could we weather this storm. Suddenly, a 20-year-old memory appeared. It was the random, out-of-the-blue question our pastor had asked me during premarital counseling, "Rick, does adultery necessitate divorce?"

I remembered telling him no. He told me I had answered correctly. He had gone on to explain that if I believed it

CHAPTER 6: THE BETRAYAL

automatically meant divorce, then I, in essence, would be saying that God was not big enough to heal and restore a marriage. I realized that question might not have been as random and out-of-the-blue after all. With that memory now fresh in my mind, I went to sleep.

The next morning, Eric and I went for a drive in the mountains. He simply loved on me with a listening ear as I wept off and on. He let me know he needed to call Don Smith, our district supervisor, to let him know what had happened. I knew he needed to make arrangements immediately for our church. I could hear Don's sadness through the phone.

He asked if Tiffany and I would be willing to speak with Dr. Ted and Diane Roberts of Pure Desire Ministries. Without thinking, I said yes, but I was not sure in that moment. Eric called Dr. Ted on my behalf since I was a blubbering mess and couldn't speak. Dr. Ted told Eric to have me call him in the next few days if Tiffany and I wanted to meet with him and Diane.

That afternoon, Eric and I took in a movie to help distract me from my thoughts. I could not sit through the movie I had chosen. It did not have romance or anything inappropriate, but the plotline happened to have the element of an affair, causing me to experience trigger after trigger.

At one point, Eric asked me if I wanted to leave. I think I stood up even before I answered yes. As we left that theater, I noticed an attractive woman walking toward me as she headed toward one of the other theaters.

Since I thought things might be over between Tiffany and me, I said to myself, "She's pretty. I guess I may be back on the market here shortly and I can pursue a woman like that." But, just as fast as that *sad* thought came, I said under my breath, only for me to hear, "But I don't want that lady. I want my wife!"

When we got back in the car, my phone went off. A text from Tiffany. It was the first contact we had since I left the night before. Her text read, "I'm sorry I was unfaithful to you. You didn't deserve my betrayal. It was wrong, and I take full responsibility."

I was relieved she was at least admitting what she had done was wrong; it seemed like the polar opposite of her defensive attitude the night before. Her text communicated a sense of sorrow and vulnerability. Before I responded, Eric and I chatted about this new emotional state Tiffany might be in.

Out of the blue I blurted out, "She's still my wife!" It was at that moment I realized I did not want to let go and throw away our 20 years of marriage. That realization led me to pray silently, "I guess I'm more willing, Lord, than I thought." Just like the night before, the Holy Spirit immediately whispered to me, "You and Tiffany provide the heart; I'll provide the miracle!"

At that exact moment, the peace that surpasses all understanding that Paul wrote about in Philippians 4:7 overcame me. There was a supernatural hope deposited in my heart. I could breathe somewhat easier and actually sense a light ever so vaguely starting to show itself in this darkest of time in my life. Tiffany and I began to text back and forth that day, which led to me returning home that evening.

When I got back to our house, Tiffany was sitting in the living room. It was evident she had never stopped crying from the night before. Her face was puffy and her eyes were red; she looked wrecked. I sat on the end of the coffee table and just looked at her calmly.

While her face was buried in her arms that were resting on her knees, I said: "Look at me."

Full of shame she responded, "No, I don't want to."

"Please look at me," I asked again.

CHAPTER 6: THE BETRAYAL

She slowly and hesitantly glanced up, and we had eye contact. God must have begun to answer my tweet from the day before: to be made more like Him—at that moment, when our eyes met I was moved with authentic compassion for her. It was as if I was looking at Tiffany through Jesus' eyes. Suddenly, the condemnation I had felt 24 hours earlier was replaced with a broken heart for my wife. I decided not to cast a stone in her direction, but rather lay it down and follow Jesus' lead in what to do next.

"In spite of everything, I still love you," I softly told her.

"Don't say that to me. I don't deserve it," she cried.

"I do not love you because you deserve it. I love you, simply because I just do. Do you love me?"

I stared at her intently, wondering what she would say. She looked up at me with bloodshot eyes filled with tears and nodded yes. Then she blurted out, "I don't even want to be with him! I want you! These last few months I kept telling Lauren that it was not good for their family to come up and visit. I told her that because I was ending the stupid affair; I wanted it to end!"

I took a deep breath and just looked at her. "What do you want to do now? Do you want to work things out and try to restore our marriage?"

With heavy breathing and tears flowing down her cheeks, she nodded yes.

"Okay, I'm really glad to know that, because I would like to work things out as well."

The next morning, we were getting ready to take our daughter to her basketball tournament down south. As Tiffany stood in our closet looking for something to wear, I walked up behind her, put both hands on her shoulders, gave her a gentle squeeze, and kissed the top of her head. She did not turn around but immediately started crying.

"I'm ashamed," she stated. "I'm not deserving of forgiveness."

As I let go and started to walk away, I told her, "None of us are deserving of forgiveness."

I was not scheduled to teach that Sunday at church, which made things a little easier for Don, my district supervisor, as he began sorting things out for the following Sunday. However, on Monday we needed to connect with him to talk about next steps.

HEART CHECK

We do not have a high priest who is unable to empathize with our weaknesses, but we have One who has been tempted in every way, just as we are—yet He did not sin.

HEBREWS 4:15

// 1. Who or what makes you feel valued and loved?

_____
_____
_____
_____
_____
_____

// 2. Are there snags in your relationship that never change? List those things.

_____
_____
_____
_____
_____
_____
_____

// 3. **What would bring hope in believing these snags could change?**

_____
_____
_____
_____
_____

// 4. **What steps can *you* take to begin to hope for change?**

_____
_____
_____
_____
_____

// 5. **Think about and write down potential snags that exist in your relationship that may be caused because *you* are choosing to die on a hill or dig your heels in.**

_____
_____
_____
_____
_____

CHAPTER 7

ROAD TO RECOVERY, PART 1
CAN'T WALK IT ALONE

TIFFANY: Rick and I spoke with Don on Monday. He lovingly let me know he was disappointed in my actions but would be there for Rick and me and help in any way he could. He informed me that Rick would have to step down immediately from his position as senior pastor. Honestly, I was sad and relieved. I was sad because I knew I had caused Rick to lose his dream job, but relieved because my secret was out: he and I could finally focus on *us* getting healed. Don told us that the following Sunday he would come to our church and break the news to the congregation.

RICK: Before the congregation heard the news, I had to share it with my church council and staff with Don present. They were saddened and surprised, asking: "Did you see this coming?" "How could she have done this and led worship all this time?" "You couldn't have been that bad of a husband to cause her to do this; were you?" And the questions kept coming. These were honest, heartfelt questions that were asked out of pain and confusion.

I answered them the best I could. One statement within a question stuck out to me: "You couldn't have been that bad of a husband to cause her to do this." I knew what the person meant. Although not excusing Tiffany's actions, he was asking if I had contributed to the division in our marriage that allowed her to fall into this trap more easily.

I immediately and naïvely answered, "Not at all." However, I did not consider the emotional abuse she endured whenever I had said, "You're an embarrassment to me," "You're crazy," or "If I fail in ministry, it will be because of you." I also never considered my neglectful behavior of not caring for our home and putting my work before family. I would learn through our counseling that I had been completely blinded to the turmoil and destruction I caused in our marriage for the last 20 years.

Don informed the council and my staff what was going to happen with the church, at least for the time being. He told them he was open to the idea of me being reinstated, but at the moment that decision was far from being determined.

Tiffany and I reached out to Dr. Ted and Diane Roberts of Pure Desire Ministries. We made an appointment to meet at their office in Gresham, Oregon, for an evaluation. However, there were a few tests we needed to take before our initial visit. We both had to take an assessment that revealed how closely or *far apart* each of us viewed our marriage in comparison to each other. Tiffany had to take an analysis to uncover any addictive behaviors she might be struggling with, as well as answer a questionnaire regarding her current psychological state. These evaluations would determine the type of treatment she would need. During the few days before we drove to Pure Desire Ministries, things were copacetic between the two of us.

CHAPTER 7: ROAD TO RECOVERY, PART I

TIFFANY: Before we made the six-hour drive south to Gresham, Oregon, we had some unfinished business to deal with on the home front. The dust had settled. Josh was in a much better place emotionally and was able to speak cordially to me. Rick and I told him we were going to share what had happened with his brothers and sister because we did not want him to carry the burden of knowing something so big all by himself. We wanted him to have the freedom to speak with his siblings if he felt he needed to ease his heart or flush out his feelings. Josh very much appreciated that.

As we began to share with our children individually, it felt like pouring Bactine on a wound; it stung badly! Kaleb, age 20, immediately broke down and cried, asking the same questions Josh did. Jared, age 15, did not cry but visibly was hurt and angry and asked the same questions his older brothers did. Faith, age 11, just said, "Oh." But over the next couple years, she realized the seriousness of what happened.

It was now out in the open, *within our immediate family*. We did what we could to console our children and let them know we were going to try to work things out. I often cried and asked for forgiveness from our kids. I was ashamed and had sincere remorse for the pain I had caused our whole family.

We made the trip to Pure Desire Ministries. Rick and I sat in the waiting room for our appointment with Dr. Ted and Diane Roberts. We were both nervous, not knowing what was going to happen, especially as we waited to hear the results of the online questionnaires we had filled out days earlier.

Our meeting began with basic introductions. Dr. Ted asked how we were doing that day. He and Diane spoke healing words of grace and mercy, all with a non-judgmental heart. We felt loved on, safe, and encouraged. It was truly the first time we saw a glimmer of white light piercing through the darkest time in our marriage. They were like world-renowned surgeons in the ER giving life back to two corpses. They cried and laughed with us. We witnessed right before our eyes what Paul meant in Galatians 6:2 about carrying each other's burdens. Dr. Ted and Diane, through sincerity, began walking with us in a partnership way.

The results of the questionnaires we had filled out revealed a sad reality concerning the state of our marriage. Dr. Ted pointed out that after 20-plus years of marriage, we had completely polar opposite views of our relationship. I remember he looked at Rick and said, "You don't know your wife. You're clueless about the true state of your marriage."

Rick was shocked, but he did not disagree. Dr. Ted went on to explain that we were not on the same page, *at any level*. To further Dr. Ted's point, I asked Rick right then and there if he was aware of how long I had not worn my wedding ring because it was broken. He was surprised when I said it had been five years. I asked him if he thought I was upset that I couldn't wear it. Because he was not in touch with me, he thought I wasn't all that bothered by it.

This small example highlighted how out of touch Rick was with my feelings and our relationship as a whole. The two of us also learned that I was not a "sex addict" but closer to a "love addict." The difference is that a sex addict's life is typically interrupted and disrupted by a habitual obsession for sex; it is very compulsory. The love addict is fueled and intoxicated by the rush of being pursued, cared for, and drawn to anything remotely romantic.

Knowing myself, I am a real romantic at heart and craved being pursued by Rick. The final questionnaire revealed that, even though I had a moral failure, I apparently still possessed enough confidence in myself regarding who I was in Christ and

CHAPTER 7: ROAD TO RECOVERY, PART I

as a person. Dr. Ted said that meant that with proper counseling I could be a strong and supportive wife to Rick *if* God called him back into the senior pastor role.

He then looked at Rick and told him he would be out of ministry for a minimum of six months. This timeline depended on how well we were doing in our recovery process. Rick was encouraged to find work elsewhere, which he did.

We spent about two to three hours with Dr. Ted and Diane. We both felt it was time well spent. They said that if we decided to pursue their yearlong counseling program, I would be required to take a polygraph test.

Dr. Ted explained that by doing so in the beginning of our counseling, Rick would get down to the bottom of the barrel and find out everything he needed to forgive. Once he knew that, Rick could decide if he wanted to move forward in our marriage.

He went on to explain there is nothing worse than getting six months into recovery and finding out something else that might be a deal-breaker for the other spouse. It was better to discover every ugly thing upfront and know what one is dealing with rather than having something surface later.

Dr. Ted let Rick know that the recovery process is full of triggers he would experience. But over time, they would happen less frequently. He told Rick that if I passed the polygraph test, he could use the results as an anchor for himself whenever he experienced doubt and/or triggers.

Because I had already shared everything with Rick, I immediately said, "I'll do it! He knows everything. I have nothing to hide." Rick told me that my willingness surprised him, while at the same time provided comfort.

Dr. Ted and Diane were pleased to see my readiness to take the polygraph test and told Rick this was a good sign. A couple of weeks later, I took the test at the Sheriff's Department in Vancouver, Washington.

When it was over, the deputy told Rick, "She's not hiding anything; *know that*. She was honest and transparent, and nothing showed that she was lying and then tried to correct her answers."

Looking at both of us, he said, "This is something the two of you should celebrate." Rick appreciated the comment and was thankful. We felt like we were on the road to recovery and Jesus was keeping His promise: "You provide the willing hearts, and I'll provide the miracle."

RICK: We immediately began to see the miracle of God's hand in our restoration process. I decided to share what was going on with my parents. Their hearts were broken for us. They were saddened by Tiffany's choice to have an affair, but they still declared their love for her. They comforted me with words of encouragement and told me they were in a financial position to help us and wanted to cover the cost of our counseling. Tiffany and I were humbled by their generosity.

Over the next six months, we met with Dr. Ted and Diane once a week for two hours via Google Hangout. Eventually, we switched to twice-a-month meetings. We spent the first hour talking about how things were going, and we navigated through the book *The Genesis Process* by Michael Dye.[5]

During the second hour, we'd separate. Tiffany would spend time with Diane going through the book, *Pure Desire for Women:*

---

5. Dye, M. (2012). *The Genesis Process: For Change Groups, Book 1 and 2, Individual Workbook*. Ventura, CA: Michael Dye.

CHAPTER 7: ROAD TO RECOVERY, PART I

Eight Pillars to Freedom.[6] Dr. Ted met with me, and we went through the book, *Hope for Men, Healing for Broken Trust*.[7]

In addition to our time with them, Tiffany was part of a women's support and accountability group that met every Monday evening for two hours via Google Hangout. Together they went through the *Eight Pillars to Freedom* book.

Through our yearlong counseling, Tiffany and I experienced extreme highs and extreme lows as we walked through our recovery process. It was anything but easy. I was learning about triggers and initially was not handling them well. It seemed everything was a trigger. Everything reminded me of what Tiffany had done, and that put me into a tailspin.

I'm sad to say that during those moments, my sarcastic side came out in a verbally abusive way. There were times when Tiffany texted Diane and Dr. Ted in between our regularly scheduled meetings to ask if one of them could reach out and help me process a trigger I was experiencing.

The triggers were powerful for the first year (or two). As time went on, I was taught how to handle them and not lash out— something we will share more on in Chapter 14: Discovering the Right Tools. Eventually, the triggers became few and far between. I'm happy to say that I rarely have them today.

Many times I wondered if I could handle the recovery process. The betrayal challenged my resolve. I was literally learning that Jesus' statement about forgiveness in Matthew 18:22 meant to do so over and over and over again.

---

6. Roberts, D. (2010). *Pure Desire for Women: Eight Pillars to Freedom from love addiction & sexual issues*. Gresham, OR: Pure Desire Ministries International.
7. Roberts, T. & Roberts, D. (2012). *Hope For Men: Healing for Broken Trust*. Gresham, OR: Pure Desire Ministries International.

Forgiveness was and is a daily choice, and depending on the day, it was sometimes an hourly decision I had to make. It was painful to do because of the deep hurt I felt. Tim Keller once tweeted, "Repentance is like antiseptic. You pour antiseptic onto a wound and, at first, it stings. Then it heals."[8] Even though it was painful, the more I chose to forgive Tiffany, the more healing it brought to our relationship.

As I realized it took great strength to forgive my wife, I internally was struggling to forgive my friend, Chad. He was now nobody to me. I would rather kick him to the curb and forget about him than tell him I forgave him. I had no plans ever to engage him in any way. But, in the course of our recovery, I knew in the back of my mind there would be a day when the Lord would call me to forgive *even him*, the man with whom my wife had an affair.

I would tell myself, "One step at a time," as I pushed this idea farther down the road.

TIFFANY: Early on in our counseling, I asked if it was normal for me to be further along than Rick in the area of feeling good about everything. It felt like he was a little behind me in the recovery process. I wanted to know how worried I should be.

Rick had noticed the same thing—that he was struggling a bit more than me—and was glad I asked that question.

Diane said, "Of course you're feeling better more quickly than Rick. Think about it. The weight of the affair that you had been carrying for more than three years has now been lifted, which provides you with great relief. However, that weight has

---

8. Keller, T. (2015). Original Tweet: January 11. Retrieved from https://twitter.com/timkellernyc.

CHAPTER 7: ROAD TO RECOVERY, PART I

now been transferred onto Rick. He's now carrying the weight of *your* betrayal."

We both had an "ah-ha" moment. I immediately looked at Rick and repented. I realized he now had to carry the weight of my sin through his recovery process. He again graciously forgave me.

Our counseling sessions were not always easy. Sometimes Rick got a little amped up as he tried to convey his emotions concerning a particular issue. And I had my moments as well.

One time, I just got up and walked out of our first hour with Dr. Ted and Diane. I did come back; however, I did not want to because the discussion we were having was too upsetting for me.

Counseling is a good thing but a painful experience at times. It feels like you're going to the doctor to have him inspect a wound that is painful, but in doing so, the doctor (counselor) has to touch areas that are still raw and injured. Rick and I had to learn to be okay with this; it was part of the necessary process to bring complete healing and restoration to our marriage.

RICK: Tiffany and I personally know a couple who experienced something similar to us. However, they decided to take a different route for their healing. They chose *not* to pursue counseling. Instead they went on vacation after vacation trying to insert fun into their relationship with the hope of manufacturing a new romance between them.

This sweep-it-under-the-rug approach only allowed them to minimize the sting of the affair, but ultimately gloss over the root cause for why it happened in the first place. This method, albeit more fun and less confrontational, is more of a Band-Aid fix that does not deal with the root issues in their marriage.

This shallow approach to overcome their tragic experience could make them susceptible to repeat the transgression that caused damage to their relationship. And, if by chance they do not experience the moral failure again, their relationship will never be truly healed the way the Lord intended it to be.

One thing I have learned through our counseling is that Jesus wants to deal with our sin head-on. He's not really into quick fixes or sweeping things under the rug. In fact, we see Him deal directly with the sin of the woman at the well in John 4:16–17. Jesus "told her, 'Go, call your husband and come back.' 'I have no husband,' she replied. Jesus said to her, 'You are right when you say you have no husband. The fact is, you have had five husbands, and the man you now have is not your husband.'"

Lovingly, Jesus confronted her sinful past, as well as her present. Jewish tradition allowed someone to get married up to three different times; she's beyond five! Jesus wanted to work in her life, but He first needed to deal with the sin in her life.

Like most people, she was not having it and actually tried changing the topic of conversation. People typically do not like confronting their sin. They do not want to walk through the pain of their poor decisions and instead just want to forget about it, but that's not healthy. We've learned that counseling is not for wimps. It takes guts to be vulnerable and allow someone to get into your business. It is painful, but if done right, it's profitable!

Proverbs 28:13 says, "Whoever conceals their sins does not prosper, but the one who confesses and renounces them finds mercy." Tiffany and I found this verse to be true. Being transparent with our mistakes, doing the hard, painful work through counseling, instead of concealing it and not dealing with it, we found mercy and forgiveness that allowed us to step into new freedom as a married couple—freedom we've always longed for.

HEART CHECK

*Where there is no counsel, the people fall;
but in the multitude of counselors **there is** safety.*
PROVERBS 11:14 (NKJV)

// 1. Who do you go to when you need a safe place to share your deepest thoughts, actions, or deeds?

_____

_____

// 2. Does this person tell you what you *want to hear* or do they minister *truth in love* that evokes a heart check from you?

_____

_____

// 3. Do you have an accountability partner you meet with regularly? ☐ Yes ☐ No

// 4. Do you have a mentor who helps you grow emotionally and spiritually? ☐ Yes ☐ No

// 5. Do you and your spouse meet with someone who helps you in *marriage maintenance*? ☐ Yes ☐ No

// 6. Do you and your spouse meet with someone who helps you with *parenting issues*? ☐ Yes ☐ No

// 7. Out of questions 3, 4, 5, and 6, which one can you address immediately and why?

_____
_____
_____
_____

// 8. Describe how your life displays vulnerability and transparency.

_____
_____
_____
_____

// 9. List the areas in your life where biblical counseling would help bring resolve to you, your spouse, and your family.

_____
_____
_____
_____
_____

CHAPTER 8

ROAD TO RECOVERY, PART 2
CONNECTING THE DOTS

RICK: I will take on writing this chapter, and you'll see why as you read on. I remember my Kindergarten teacher giving us coloring books. I'd search for the Connect the Dots pages; I loved doing them. I always first looked at a page with dots all over it and tried to see the completed picture. Most of the time, it wasn't until I started connecting the dots that the image began to take shape. Connecting the dots gradually brought about clarity and I eventually saw the picture for what it was.

Counseling was a lot like this for Tiffany and me. Dr. Ted and Diane helped us connect the dots in our lives, which revealed the real picture of our relationship. They guided us through conversation after conversation highlighting dots that needed to be connected, which provided a better understanding in the areas where we were struggling. For Tiffany and me, this *real-life game* of Connect the Dots allowed us not only to see the true picture of our marriage, but also why there were so many conflicts between us that ultimately drove a wedge in our relationship.

In the beginning, I was ridiculously naïve when it came to our counseling. I approached our time together arrogantly, thinking that we'd finally get down to the bottom of *Tiffany's issues*. I believed counseling would get her sorted out.

Within the first few sessions with Dr. Ted and Diane, I realized that not only were we going to be learning about Tiffany, but I would also discover my *blind spots*:[9] dots in my life that needed to be revealed and dealt with as they played a serious role in the division we had in our relationship. Yes, Tiffany did have her issues. She had an anger problem that seemed to be passed down from generation to generation. Tiffany could be a little OCD, and it was difficult for her to receive constructive criticism. However, she did not have anything significant happen to her growing up. There was no major childhood trauma, such as:

- She was not sexually violated.
- She did not have an absent father.
- Her parents were not verbally or physically abusive.
- She was not neglected or abandoned.
- She was not a partier in high school.
- She was not sexually active as a teen.

Tiffany was fortunate to not have to deal with these issues in her backstory. What is very *unfortunate* about the above issues is that those experiences quite often have a significant influence on people when they become an adult. *Not all the time.* But such childhood cruelty can trigger unhealthy ways of coping later in life, such as sexual sin (an affair, pornography, masturbation, etc.). Or, drive one to use alcohol or drugs (prescription or not) as a way of coping to numb-out stress or pain.

---

9. Dye, M. (2012). *The Genesis Process: For Change Groups, Book 1 and 2, Individual Workbook*. Ventura, CA: Michael Dye. 109.

CHAPTER 8: ROAD TO RECOVERY, PART 2

For all intents and purposes, Tiffany was pretty vanilla. So, it begs the question: how could someone, who had a pretty ordinary childhood, commit adultery 20 years into her marriage? This is what Dr. Ted and Diane were going to help us figure out.

In counseling, I learned more about *my problems* than I ever thought possible. It was sobering. Yes, our time together did help us learn about her unresolved issues, as well as how she became vulnerable to commit such a moral failure. (She sees her moral failure as her fault, and she owns it without excuses.) However, what led up to it was *not* solely on her—something I had to come to grips with.

Early in our time with Dr. Ted and Diane, I started to feel like I was in the middle of my very own real-life Connect the Dots game. I began to have epiphany after epiphany about myself and the role I played in damaging our marriage. When these dots were revealed and connected to actual issues we struggled with, I was stunned. I was not prepared for the real-life version of this childhood game.

After identifying the first few dots and connecting them, I humbly realized Tiffany's main problem that needed to be fixed was *me*! I did not see that coming. Dr. Ted and Diane identified dots that were blind spots for me and connected them to areas that caused trauma in our relationship. They had to point them out in order for Tiffany and me to have an accurate picture of our marriage. I wish I could have turned the page and started a new connect-the-dot game, but I could not. I knew deep down that I had to allow the counseling to play out if I wanted real healing for Tiffany and me.

Over the next 12 months of our counseling, I learned about what made me tick as a husband, along with how to successfully relate to Tiffany. Dr. Ted helped me discover that my issues, if not realized and corrected, would dampen—or even worse, stop—the restoration process between us.

Part of our counseling was that Dr. Ted and Diane were there to help Tiffany and me sort out her frustration with me. Her irritation with me, which led to anger and deep resentment toward me, played a part in her becoming disconnected emotionally, which ultimately led to her affair.

Some dots needed to be connected from *my actions* to *her* pain, but also *my actions* needed to be connected to *my past*. It was like a more in-depth version of the game: connect the dots *within* the dots, expert level. Playing the game at this level helped us get down to many root issues that brought clarity, and began to bring healing to both of us.

Together we learned things I *did* and *did not* do during the 20 years of our marriage, that became the source of Tiffany's wounds. On the surface, they may seem trivial, but because of her childhood experiences and two decades of being let down over and over again, Tiffany's confusion and minor irritations toward me turned into bitterness and resentment. The hurt she felt led her to build a false narrative about my love for her and our family.

Here are a few dots that were connected, giving us both understanding that led to healing and freedom in our marriage.

LACK OF HOME REPAIRS

Not fixing things in our home was a sore spot for Tiffany. I knew she got irritated when I didn't repair something right away. However, what I did not realize was that because her dad had cared for their home growing up, that action made her feel loved. She saw him fixing things or having them fixed right away as another way of caring for their family.

CHAPTER 8: ROAD TO RECOVERY, PART 2

When I didn't fix things or fix things in a reasonable timeframe, Tiffany viewed it as a lack of love and care for our family. Through our counseling, we learned there was a dot *within* a dot that was the root issue here.

My procrastination was not about a lack of love, but rather stemmed from my childhood insecurity in fixing things. I could trace my self-doubt back to my dad not realizing that every time I suggested how to fix something he'd say lovingly and kindly, "No Ricky, just watch; you'll learn."

When something broke in our home, like the towel bar in the bathroom, my insecurity kicked in immediately, and I got stressed. I was overwhelmed by the idea of having to potentially fix the drywall (because one of our kids yanked the bar off the wall). As lame as this may sound, I shut down emotionally and put off fixing the towel bar. I'd rather buy a towel rack for the back of the door and say, "Hang your towels here!" But then I still wouldn't fix the towel bar, or I'd take six to nine months to finally get around to it.

Dr. Ted told me I needed to renew my mind in this area, step up, and start getting things done. He explained, I could not continue to allow insecurity to get in the way of not caring for our family in this manner. Now that I was aware of why I put off household repairs, it was up to me to do the responsible thing and change my behavior.

LACK OF CAR UPKEEP

Growing up, Tiffany could count on her dad to be very diligent regarding the maintenance of not only his car but hers as well. Just about every weekend, all the hoods were up on all the vehicles while her dad checked the fluids to make sure everything was okay. He also checked the tires and washed the windshield. Since Tiffany's love language is Acts of Service, nothing seemed to say "I love you" more to her than the kind gesture of her dad checking on her car.

When it came to our cars, I was diligent about getting the oil changed every 3,000 miles and putting gas in them, but unfortunately, that's where I stopped. I never checked the oil or the tires. I rarely washed our cars. To do so was never on my radar. Hold onto your seat: we're about to have another ah-ha, dot-connecting-*within*-a-dot, moment.

In counseling, I shared that my first car was brand new, so I never worried about checking the oil. And, living in the desert—and especially having dirt as a driveway—one might only wash their car when it got filthy on the outside, and that at a car wash. And, said person would almost regret cleaning it as they pulled back into their dirt yard. Dr. Ted and Diane helped Tiffany see that my lack of initiative was not because I didn't love her. It was because I grew up differently.

What's interesting is that the two of us never discovered this about each other for 20 years. Tiffany had an *unspoken rule* tucked in her heart that the husband, just about weekly, should maintain the vehicles, as well as keep them clean. I, as her husband, did not grow up doing that, so it was not on my radar. The enemy capitalized on her misunderstanding of my motivation (or lack of it) in this area, and over time, he used it to stir the pot of division in our marriage.

LACK OF YARD MAINTENANCE

If my lack of fixing things and washing cars was not enough, another sore spot for Tiffany that turned into total bewilderment

CHAPTER 8: ROAD TO RECOVERY, PART 2

was my lack of yard maintenance. Tiffany's father was diligent about keeping their yard in good shape. It always looked nice and presentable. It was common to see her dad pulling a weed here and there, or mowing and edging their lawn. Again, to a little girl growing up, this spoke volumes to her as it made her feel cared for. She interpreted these moments as her dad not wanting them to live trashy but have a beautiful home.

When I didn't do these things, allowed the weeds to pop up and begin to take over, Tiffany wondered why I didn't care enough to maintain our home. Did I not care about the environment our family was living in? That was not it at all. However, like my inattentiveness with our cars, there were dots *within* the dots that needed to be connected for Tiffany (and me) to understand what was actually going on.

Living in the desert during my childhood, my dad took care of our yard. From time to time, he'd have me join him in maintaining it. But this is where the turning point happened for me. Growing up, part of the brilliant side of my punishments when I was on restriction was being made to go outside and do yard work. This was a parenting technique Tiffany and I adopted from my mom and dad with our kids.

However, for me, pulling weeds or doing yard work of any kind came to be viewed as a punishment rather than a responsibility. As an adult, I saw yard work as a sentence; therefore, I despised doing it. It was something I put off because, in a weird way, I felt like I was in trouble when I did it.

Counseling helped me sort out this faulty way of thinking, and it provided Tiffany with some insight—that my lack of yard work wasn't because I didn't care for the family. We both had a connecting-the-dots, ah-ha moment. Like the issue of not fixing things around the home, Dr. Ted challenged me to take my new understanding and not waste it, but instead change my mentality and go pull weeds, to which I said, "Yes, sir." Today, I enjoy doing yard work; I find it very therapeutic.

NOT LOCKING UP AT NIGHT

This particular topic for Tiffany was a big issue; it seemed to speak the loudest to her. Since the very beginning of our marriage, she was the one who locked up our home. She checked every window making sure it was shut and secured. She made her rounds to every door, confirming all were closed and locked.

Before making her way to bed, she walked through the house, looking for any lit candles. I'm embarrassed to say that I never did these safety checks. My lack of initiative toward keeping our family safe *in this way* spoke volumes to Tiffany. She often asked herself, "Why doesn't Rick want to do this for our family? Does he really not care about our safety?"

Looking back, I don't blame Tiffany for wondering such things. A wife wants to feel like her husband is the family's protector. She wants to feel their surroundings are safe and secure from all harm. For two decades, I let her do what I should have been doing, which resulted in her losing respect for me at a deep level.

In counseling, she shared that her dad did what she was doing for their family every night. As a little girl, she naturally assumed that when she got married someday, her husband would do this.

Here was another opportunity for Dr. Ted and Diane to help us connect the dots. They asked why I allowed Tiffany to lock up every night. Not to give excuses, but I shared that we never locked our doors when I was growing up. Where we lived in the 70s and early 80s, it was safe. In fact, my dad always left the key

CHAPTER 8: ROAD TO RECOVERY, PART 2

in the ignition of his green Dodge pickup truck parked in the driveway. This was not just a Bulman thing to do either. All my friends' homes were always unlocked. It was not on my radar as a significant thing that needed to be done by the husband, or at all.

I went on to explain that when we got married, Tiffany asked me to lock up, but I told her we were fine and there was no threat to our kids or us. I naïvely told her she could lock up if she wanted, but there was no real need to do so. And, over time I just got accustomed to her doing it and didn't think anything of it. It was not until almost 20 years of marriage that I discovered this was a way bigger deal than I realized and how emotionally damaging it was to my wife.

Tiffany, with the help of Dr. Ted and Diane, saw that it was not that I didn't care, but rather I was just shockingly absent-minded regarding this issue. I look back on this and can't believe how blinded I was. Even if I didn't understand why something was important to Tiffany, as her husband, who was called to love her as Christ loved the church, I should have stepped up and just served her in this way. Doing so would have safeguarded our relationship that much more.

WORKAHOLIC

Tiffany always felt she competed with my work. She continually found herself vying for my time, but too often lost out to my customers, my employees, and just other people in general. As I got older, I realized I had this driven side of me. It was like I'd get so focused on something, I couldn't give attention to other important things, *like family*.

If I was winning at work and making great money, I viewed it as a positive for my entire household. Tiffany and I did not have to worry about money, which *seemed like a good thing*. We had a newly built home with an oversize cul-de-sac for the kids to play in, which *seemed like a good thing*. We could afford brand new cars, which *seemed like a good thing*. And, we went on family vacations, which *seemed like a good thing*. I saw the fruit of my hard work bringing fun and freedom to our family.

Dr. Ted and Diane helped me connect the dots to what I thought I was doing for my family versus the real effect it had. Vacations were great, but I didn't see that I spoiled their fun because I'd break away for an hour or more every day to work.

My kids wanted me to play with them, but even on vacation, I interrupted playtime with work. The financial freedom, our home, cars, and trips were not as appreciated because Tiffany and the kids felt neglected by me and put in second position. I was blind to this reality. I thought that because I was providing in a materialistic way, I was doing a good job, when in fact, I was losing—losing big time!

For most of our first 20 years, I was a workaholic. That coupled with Tiffany and me tearing each other down with our words, each of us being unaware of *unspoken rules*, and then combined with our childhood influences, led to monumental misunderstandings. This caused a horrific division in our marriage. We were a recipe for disaster, and the enemy had a field day with us.

Playing a real-life version of Connect the Dots in counseling helped me see that my unsavory behavior damaged the most important person in my life: *my wife*. I began to recognize my abuse and neglect for what it was, immoral and sinful behavior that was a violation of God's statute for how men are supposed to treat their wives.

CHAPTER 8: ROAD TO RECOVERY, PART 2

There were many times I interrupted Dr. Ted when I realized what I had been doing. "Oh, my gosh," I'd say, "I'm guilty of this (*stating a particular behavior we were discussing*)," and it crushed me. I betrayed Tiffany, but *just in a different way* than she betrayed me. Through counseling, I finally grasped that truth.

I began to own this new information I was learning about myself. Ultimately, I didn't blame myself for Tiffany's affair. Yes, I was a subpar husband in many respects, but it did not and never would justify her betrayal.

She owned her sin as a willful decision she made to help fill the hole in her damaged heart. She believes that a sinful act to fill a void is never justifiable and always wrong. I still held her responsible for her actions, but I did realize that maybe—just maybe—if I had not betrayed her in my own way for so long, she may have been in a better place emotionally to withstand the advances of another man. She could have felt like a confidently loved wife who was consistently and emotionally filled with love by her husband. This possibility could have made the difference in her choices with Chad.

HEART CHECK

And you shall know the truth, and the truth shall make you free.
JOHN 8:32 (NKJV)

// 1. Write your true thoughts about how you feel about yourself and explain "why" you think or feel this way.

_____
_____
_____
_____
_____
_____
_____
_____
_____

// 2. What belief system did you create in your earlier years of life? Answer the following questions:

- I must always _____
- I must always _____
- I must never _____
- I must never _____

// 3. What behaviors did you develop that helped you cope with life (i.e., drinking, eating, use of Internet, working)?

_____
_____
_____
_____

// 4. How did these behaviors affect you:

- Mentally: _____
- Spiritually: _____
- Emotionally: _____
- Physically: _____
- Socially: _____

// 5. After completing this exercise, what area(s) do you see you need to change?

_____
_____
_____
_____
_____
_____
_____
_____
_____

CHAPTER 9

RETURNING TO THE CHURCH
FACING THE MUSIC

RICK: Having to face my staff and council at our church and share what had happened to our family was beyond difficult. It was at that moment I truly realized that one's sin could have a tragic ripple effect that touches and potentially destroys the hearts of many. When sitting down with Don Smith (my district supervisor) and my council, I witnessed what seemed like a heavy blanket of sorrow being laid on all who were present. Many of them were asking understandably tough and heartfelt questions:

- Why didn't we see this coming?
- Rick, how could you have not known that something was off in your marriage?
- How could Tiffany have led worship yet lived a life of duplicity?
- How could you be fooled by her betrayal?

These were honest questions asked lovingly and kindly—questions I did not necessarily have comforting answers for. I sat there that evening, realizing that my family's sin had directly changed the life narrative of each person who attended our church. Their story now has the mark of an affair on it, even though they had nothing to do with the sin. It hurt to walk away, knowing I might never be back.

After the sixth month of therapy with Dr. Ted and Diane, they decided Tiffany and I were healthy enough to return to our church and shared that information with Don and the council, who had eagerly been awaiting the green light. However, Dr. Ted and Diane recommended that Tiffany sit out of ministry and leading for another year.

I was blown away. "God, are You really doing this for me? For us?" I asked Him this many times leading up to our reinstallation service. I was humbled by the grace and gift to serve wonderful people again.

Returning to my role was an interesting experience for me, but gut-wrenching for Tiffany. I asked her often if she was okay with me resuming my position as senior pastor because that meant she had to face all the people who knew her darkest and dirtiest secret. Her willingness to come back and support me, facing the congregation she hurt, blew my mind.

I am not sure I would have been strong enough, courageous enough, or selfless enough to come back. Tiffany did not know if people would embrace her. She didn't know if they would genuinely forgive and love her.

Some people may think, "It's the church. Of course they'll be kind, forgiving, and non-judgmental." Unfortunately, that's not always true. In some cases, the church misses the boat when it comes to caring for their own. In the words of a friend of mine, "Sometimes the church shoots their wounded."

Tiffany and I believed the congregation we served wouldn't do that, and we are happy to say that they did not. However, it was not easy as we were a church family now having to work through a myriad of emotions together.

CHAPTER 9: RETURNING TO THE CHURCH

Our church was told to give us space to heal as a family, and they did. After six months, we came back for my reinstallation service. We stood together before the congregation and Tiffany asked for forgiveness. There were mixed emotions in the room that we learned about over the next few months. Some people thought it was great and could see Jesus at work and were celebrating what was happening.

Others expressed confusion as they wanted to hear about our journey for the last six months, something we did not share that evening. Some people were upset because they started to experience thoughts and feelings they had not anticipated having. Here are things we heard from people over the next few months as the church desperately tried to heal and regain momentum:

- "I thought I'd be okay seeing the two of you back, but it's harder than I realized."
- "It's great you got help and healing for six months, but what about all of us? We needed counseling too."
- "To be honest, I'm struggling to receive from you again. It's like I've lost respect because your family was out of order and you didn't know it."
- "I'm struggling because I'm not seeing anything different with your family. You look happy now, but you seemed happy back then. How do I know things are better?"
- "How come Tiffany isn't as outgoing as she was before?"

We don't blame the wonderful people we served for their feelings and thoughts, even though it was tough to hear when they shared. They were grieving and dealing with all sorts of heartache: shock, disbelief, anger, deep sadness, confusion, distrust. They were hurting due to the trauma *we caused*. How could we not be patient with them? They needed to be honest and flush out their emotions; something we respected.

Just because the Lord was giving me another chance at pastoring, it did not mean it was going to be easy. Over the next 18 months, I learned a ton.

One major lesson was to pastor and do what I love, but in a way where my family came first. For me, it was a different way of behaving and organizing my time so that my wife and kids didn't feel in second position to my work.

The church never did get back to the attendance figures we had enjoyed before all of our stuff came out, but that's okay—and I'm at peace with that. Why? Because of the restoration we as a church family experienced. Yes, people saw the enemy at work, but *more importantly*, they witnessed the gracious hand of God restoring one couple and their family, when most couples and families dissolve.

Our congregation saw a healthy way to deal with sin—not covering it up, but instead, tackling it and dealing with the consequences. You confess the wrongdoing, ask for forgiveness, and are willing to journey down the long road to *earn* trust back.

I'm convinced the Lord opened the door for Tiffany and me to come back to our church. He desired that His people not just be robbed by tragedy, but also be given an opportunity to celebrate His work at restoring a couple and their family. It also gave people the opportunity to extend grace and forgiveness in a way that brought Him glory.

Unfortunately, it is far too common for sin (like ours) to destroy a congregation and not allow the people the ability to experience the healing of broken friendships due to betrayal. But God is good!

CHAPTER 9: RETURNING TO THE CHURCH

TIFFANY: The day had come for Rick and me to go back to our church. I had never experienced anything in life that scared me as much as the evening of Rick's reinstallation service. Through my whole ordeal, I realized there are two ways to deal with sin: one, sweep it under the rug and move on in hopes to make the future better, or two, own the transgression and face the music.

For my marriage to be truly healed, my family restored, and the wrong done to many innocent people (our congregation) righted, I needed to do the latter. I realized that for authentic healing to take place, tough decisions need to be made and carried out. I knew I had to stand before our church family, repent, and ask for their forgiveness. It is what Jesus wanted, and the people deserved an apology.

Someone asked me what I was thinking and feeling when we drove to the church to face the people for the first time. I was super scared. Everyone there knew the worst thing I had ever done. To get a glimpse of what I felt, imagine going to your church on a Sunday knowing there was going to be an announcement in the bulletin about your worst sin for all to see—your deepest darkest secret revealed to everyone. If you're sick to your stomach at that thought, then you're getting close to how I felt.

I remember I was calm when getting ready to go that evening. However, once we got in the car, my anxiety level went from a 0 to 500. And the closer we got to the church I began to panic and feel physically sick. I began to shake. I felt like I was going to throw up. I started to cry and then struggled to regain my composure. When I got out of the car to walk inside, I felt like I could not move. I was frozen in fear. As I got out of the car, a couple in the parking lot greeted me, but because of the fog of emotion I was engulfed in, I was only able to nod. I was not able to focus, let alone hear what they were saying. When I walked into the foyer, I lost it.

What made it easier is that people came up to me and were friendly. Some embraced me with a hug to provide a sense of comfort. Most people exhibited grace and forgiveness, instead of just standing at a distance staring at me, leaving me to wonder what they were thinking. We sang a couple songs of worship to calibrate everyone's heart to be in line with the Holy Spirit. They were the longest two songs I've ever sung.

Ryan Johnson, our divisional leader, closed out our time of worship and began to share some thoughts with scripture. He did not speak long, but for me the longer, the better because I was dying inside, knowing I was about to stand before everyone and read my letter of repentance.

Ryan invited Rick and me to the platform. Before I knew it, Rick had grabbed my hand as he gently led us both to the front. We stood there before everyone. All eyes were on me, and I had never felt such vulnerability. Ryan explained what we were going to do and that it was biblical because when one person wrongs another, they are to confess their sin and ask for forgiveness. And he added that it was also biblical that as children of God, we are to extend grace and forgiveness.

Then he handed the microphone to me. At that moment, my mind went blank. I was grateful that I had written a letter to read my poignant thoughts that were from the heart. I learned later that some people were disappointed that I read my apology because they felt it didn't feel sincere.

I realize they were not aware of the degree of the emotional strain I was under. I was literally incapable of putting two thoughts together to make a coherent sentence. I was terrified to be there; I could not even walk to the back of the church to get coffee before the service started. In the end, I felt everyone extended grace to the best of their ability that evening, and I'm forever grateful.

CHAPTER 9: RETURNING TO THE CHURCH

The following weeks and months after returning to our church, it did get easier for me because I knew certain people were my allies and I felt safe around them. I knew they were *for* me. I could make eye contact and go and sit with them since I felt they had a genuine love for me.

I also knew there were people who were still struggling and did not know what to do, so they were more standoffish. They might smile in my direction, but they never really made an effort to come and say hello. I was not offended; I understood they were probably dealing with the pain and sense of betrayal I had caused.

Within the first month or so, I found out some people were disappointed that I did not walk around and mingle with folks, but instead went quietly to my seat in the front row of the sanctuary. Some just couldn't seem to understand that, for me, just getting ready and coming week after week, facing people who knew my sin, was about all I had to offer at the time. Showing up took all the courage for that day. Just to attend church, I battled the greatest level of shame. Forgiveness and healing can be messy and not always smooth—something I had to come to grips with.

What *was* comforting is that over time, these people who were standoffish one by one asked me to go for coffee. They said they wanted to check in and see how I was doing. However, I could tell they didn't only want to know how I was, they were also making an attempt to be in right relationship with me—and that was a blessing.

I knew it wasn't easy for them; they were on their own journey of healing and trying to obediently extend grace and forgiveness. There were so many wonderful women who wanted to be Jesus to me, like Margaret. This amazing lady mailed me a card once a week the entire time we were taking our break from church. And when we came back, she always demonstrated love and compassion toward me.

Then there was Joni, a grandmother who felt prompted by the Lord to write me an encouraging letter. She didn't have any paper, but what she did have was a 5 x 7 picture of her grandchildren that she kept in her Bible. That photo was all she could find to write on. She penned the most loving, kindhearted message on the back of that picture. The fact that she sacrificed the photo of her grandchildren that she kept in her Bible meant so much to me.

It was not all sunshine and rainbows. I did encounter people who spoke *out of their pain*. I had to learn to extend grace. They did not realize in those moments that the words they used caused me pain. However, just as grace had been extended to me, as hard as it was, I had to learn to be gracious and forgive them in the midst of their anger, frustration, and confusion.

This whole process of going back to our church while on my journey of redemption and recovery taught me a few lessons:

LESSON 1—TO STOP KISSING SHAME

Dr. Ted encouraged me on multiple occasions to not walk around condemned, but instead, to learn to walk forgiven: *live forgiven*. This meant to stop shaming myself for the sin I had committed. He told me that when I did that, it was like I was kissing shame, and then he'd always say, "Kissing shame is like kissing a rattlesnake; you'll get bit every time."

I had to learn to walk with my head high with the attitude of a forgiven saint and not kiss shame. For the first six months, I was successful in learning to do so with my family. However, when having to come back and face people other than my family, it challenged me and took living forgiven and not ashamed to a whole different level. It was like I had to start this discipline all

CHAPTER 9: RETURNING TO THE CHURCH

over again, but by God's grace and Rick's support, I was able to not allow shame to be my identity. Thank you, Jesus!

LESSON 2—MY SIN HAD A SHOCKWAVE EFFECT

I remember watching a video of a fertilizer plant exploding in Texas. The loud bang registered 2.1 on the Richter scale, which caused immediate annihilation at the core of the site. What was interesting is that the fertilizer plant was not the only thing affected by the explosion. Dozens of houses were instantly leveled in the area, and the shockwave shook homes as far as 50 miles away.

I learned that sin could have a similar effect. It doesn't always have an immediate impact on just one or a few people. The power of sin's explosion can be felt like a shockwave spreading throughout a community.

In my case, I quickly came to realize that my actions did not affect just my family or me; they actually had a life-impacting effect, which had the power to cause destruction to all who were close to me (friends and church family), as well as hurt people who were only acquaintances and beyond.

I realized that I was not just a person to our church family, but I was their friend, their worship leader, and the wife of their pastor, which intensified the sinful blast of my actions. I learned that I had a direct effect on many people because of the bad decisions I made.

LESSON 3—FORGIVENESS DOES NOT EQUAL TRUST

In the beginning of returning to our church, people were generously offering words of forgiveness. As time went on, I learned that forgiveness does not equal trust. I had violated trust, and that needed to be rebuilt over time. Forgiveness was people being obedient to God's Word and extending an *invitation* for an *opportunity* to restore trust with them. To be graciously given this chance to regain their confidence was a fantastic gift!

LESSON 4—MY SIN WAS A TRIGGER FOR OTHERS

Paul wrote in Romans 3:23, "For all have sinned and fall short of the glory of God." Because of this truth, people's sin can act as a flashlight that highlights the sin in others. I learned that my sin was a trigger for stuff people had not dealt with and had swept under the rug. I was also a trigger to remind them of a sin that had been committed against them.

Seeing me made it difficult for some. Possibly, I was a constant reminder of something terrible they had done or that happened to them. Triggers are awful, and people tend to have a difficult time coping with them. I was crushed to know that my sin regurgitated painful memories for some people.

LESSON 5—EVERYONE HAS THE CAPACITY TO LEAD A DOUBLE LIFE

Early in our marriage, Rick and I knew people who had committed adultery. It saddened us every time we heard it had taken place. We always looked at each other in disbelief, but I was the one who *naïvely* said, "I could never do that!"

In fact, I often asked Rick why he wouldn't declare the same sentiment, which made me nervous. He'd always say, "I think we all would like to believe we would never do something like that. The reality is that those people never planned on committing such a sin, but it happened."

He often noted that if a person was not walking with the Lord, who knows what they might do if just the right buttons

CHAPTER 9: RETURNING TO THE CHURCH

were pushed and the circumstances were perfect for this sort of thing to take place. One might not be strong enough and could have a moral failure of this nature. I saw what he was saying, but inside I was not 100 percent agreeing. But I do now!

People in our church asked, "How could Tiffany lead worship and live a life of duplicity? How could she compartmentalize such sinful behavior and serve God on Sunday?" These are great questions, and I never faulted them for asking. I think when you're living a double life, that's exactly what you're doing. You're one person when you're at church and with your family, and another person in your sin. I did feel guilty about what was going on, but somehow I learned to push that guilt aside when at church and with my family.

I was ashamed and not ready to come clean, primarily because I felt trapped and did not know how to escape or come clean. I often echoed the Apostle Paul's words in Romans 7: "Why do I do the things I don't want to do?"

My walk with the Lord was just about nonexistent, thus making it easier to live two lives. However, I missed Jesus desperately and worshiping was a way to connect with Him. Even though I was caught up in living a lie, I pushed through the guilt and led worship. I will admit that my worship was *real*, but my leading was *mechanical*. I didn't feel worthy to "lead," so I went through the motions. But worshiping in my sin actually served as an escape from it, and God was always faithful to minister personally to me as the loving Father He is. It was in those moments as I stood before our congregation that the Holy Spirit confronted me and worked on my heart.

RICK: Tiffany and I learned so much from the opportunity to come back to our church. As I led with a new perspective, putting my family first, I had to decide to sacrifice ministry for a season. The church was smaller and typically with that comes less giving. This required me to be bi-vocational. For 18 months after our return, I worked three days a week at another job and four days at the church. For a year and a half, I found myself working seven days a week.

I vowed to Tiffany that this level of commitment would only last for a season, and if things did not change and I was not able to make my way back to full-time vocational ministry, I would resign as the pastor for the betterment of our family and my health.

That day came and with a heavy, but yet obedient heart to the Lord, I decided to step down. I had to lay down my dream of senior pastoring to put my family and health first. It was a step of faith I am still walking out today as I write this portion of this chapter, more than two years after I resigned. God has been so gracious; our needs have been met, and our family continues to heal.

HEART CHECK

*People who conceal their sins will not prosper,
but if they confess and turn from them, they will receive mercy.*
PROVERBS 28:13 (NLT)

// 1. Is there any sin (behavior) in your life you have not confessed to God and others?

_____
_____
_____

// 2. How has that sin (behavior) hindered your growth in the Lord?

_____
_____
_____
_____

// 3. How do you emotionally "hide" as a result of your unconfessed actions?

_____
_____
_____

// 4. How has this sinful behavior harmed your relationships with your spouse, family, and friends?

___

// 5. What would God say to you if you stood before Him asking forgiveness for your failure?

___

// 6. Describe a time when you extended "grace" to a family member, friend, or leader who had experienced failure in his/her life.

___

CHAPTER 10

KALEB, JOSHUA, JARED, AND FAITH
FROM THE MOUTHS OF BABES

This chapter is written by our children. As a family, we had wonderful conversations around the idea of them contributing to our story. We all agreed that it made sense for all our voices to be heard as we each lived through something that was very difficult. Each one of our children experienced the same tragedy, but each internalized the family's hardship differently. They thought and processed what happened in their own way. Each one of them took the time to convey their experience of this unfortunate and regrettable incident. In the spirit of transparency, here is their story.

KALEB: When my mom's affair came out, I was not living at home. I remember on December 31, 2013, around 4:00 p.m. that my dad contacted me. He asked me to meet him in the Red Robin parking lot. I thought we were going to grab something to eat and hang out. I got into his car, and he said he needed to talk to me.

He began by saying, "Mom and I love each other very much, and no one is getting a divorce." Starting off our conversation that way helped because it provided a sense of stability in my heart concerning what I was about to hear. My dad informed me that my mom and Chad had been having an affair for that last few years. My whole life crumbled at that moment. My relationship with my mom and the health of our family suddenly seemed unreal, a sham, a total lie.

I started to cry and asked, "Why would she do that?" I was broken and distraught. What made it worse for me was that, up to that point in my life, every girl I'd dated had left me for someone else. I was beginning to struggle with trusting women because they wouldn't commit to me. This time, the most important female in my life—my mom—I felt had left me for someone else. Hearing about her affair was the "cherry on top" that sent me into a tailspin of not trusting women for the next few years.

After hearing the news about what my mom had done, it was common for me to be driving and suddenly remember everything that was going on with my family. I was filled with such anger and hurt. I felt so betrayed. My mom was the one woman I thought would never turn and stab me in the back, as most of my ex-girlfriends had done.

The biggest mistake I made was that I rushed into forgiving her. I didn't allow myself to feel the other emotions that boiled up inside of me: anger, sadness, and frustration.

About a year after finding out about her infidelity, I snapped and screamed at my mother. Standing in the driveway of our home, and not caring who was around, I shouted a name at her, one that I am too embarrassed to repeat. While this blowup saddens me, it led both of us to have a conversation that was very therapeutic for our relationship. We finally talked everything out. After we were done, it was as if a weight had been lifted off my shoulders, and I could finally start over with my mom.

Forgiving too quickly without dealing with hurt emotions is not healthy. For me, I had unresolved issues. These feelings

CHAPTER 10: KALEB, JOSHUA, JARED, AND FAITH

became an infection in my heart that began to eat at my soul, which led me to explode on my mother at the wrong place, outside in our driveway for all to hear. I should have given myself time to feel the range of different emotions that came from being betrayed. Doing so would have helped and possibly prevented me from snapping unexpectedly.

My advice to others who are affected by something similar is to be willing to forgive, but at the same time, do not neglect your hurt. Deal with the pain and sense of betrayal you are feeling, and be honest with the person who caused it. To not deal with the reality of your emotional condition is like putting a Band-Aid on a broken arm. That does nothing for the injury.

You need to get help, preferably professional help, to *reset* what is broken. A Band-Aid will only lead to greater pain down the road. It is better to deal with the reality of your situation instead of rushing through the healing process merely to get back to what you thought was "normal."

Also, when you are ready to forgive—I mean really forgive—the individual who hurt you, do so and try to move on. When someone is held captive to your bitterness, you are chained to their past behavior, and it will keep you from achieving your full potential in Christ.

Recovering from my mom's affair took awhile for me. There was a lot that my mom had to do to earn my trust. Complete transparency was vital at this time. She had to make sure her life did not come across as secretive. The most significant thing she did for me was to allow my siblings and me access to her cell phone. Whenever I wanted to check her texts, voicemails, and social media inbox messages, I could! She would never hesitate and would hand her phone to me.

Her transparency showed me that she had nothing to hide, mainly since her whole life was run through her phone. Leaving the door open for questions and my curiosity is what led me to trust her again. I am happy to say that I have completely forgiven my mother and I trust her once again. My relationship with my mom is healthy and restored, and the Lord has healed me of my inability to trust a woman.

This experience during the coldest, darkest period of my life taught me that life is not always going to be full of good seasons. This dark season gave me an opportunity to see a side of God I had never witnessed. I experienced the miraculous, mighty working hand of the Lord that was full of grace, mercy, and love for my family.

I saw Jesus restore my mom and dad's relationship. Their marriage is far from perfect, but the work that God has done and continues to do in each of them has been evident in how they approach each other as husband and wife. The fruit of God's healing power resides in our family, and to that, I say, "Thank you, Jesus!"

JOSHUA: As I sit here in my dorm room at Life Pacific University writing this portion of our family's story, I am floored by the graciousness of God and His ability to completely redeem my family.

For whatever reason, God allowed me to be there that fateful night. I was the only child present when the news of my mom's affair was revealed to my dad. I witnessed the phone call my mom received from Lauren that changed our family instantly. I watched the look on her face as Lauren yelled at her through the phone. Lauren was shouting at my mom, accusing her of having

CHAPTER 10: KALEB, JOSHUA, JARED, AND FAITH

an affair with her husband. I was standing between both of my parents when my dad's phone rang. It was Lauren calling to tell him what Chad and my mom had been doing.

Both of my parents rushed upstairs as I stayed in the family room, wondering if what was being said could be true. A million things rushed through my mind. As I made my way up the stairs to my room, I heard my parents sternly talking to one another, and then it happened. The one sign that things were wrong and everything was not okay. My dad walked out of their bedroom with a suitcase. It was at that moment I felt my heart drop. I went numb all over and immediately started to question God for the first time in my life.

My dad came into my room and very calmly talked to me. He told me it was true that my mom and Chad were having an affair. I immediately cried in disbelief. I yelled questions at my dad: "How could she do this?" "Why would she do this?" "Didn't she know this was wrong?"

Being there, seeing both of my parents' faces as my dad learned what was happening, made this experience beyond painful for me. I was 17 years old and felt I was a part of something that was way bigger than me, and I didn't know how to cope with it.

My dad talked to me for a while. He was doing his best to assure me that God was still on the throne and our only hope was to cling to Him, to lean on Him for all comfort and wisdom. I hugged my dad as we both cried. Before my dad left that evening, he made sure I was feeling a little better. Between the time he left and when I fell asleep that night, he called me on two different occasions to check in on me and pray with me. Those conversations helped lift the burden I was experiencing.

After my dad left, my mom was downstairs crying. I stood at the top of the stairwell heart-broken in disbelief at what had happened. Very quickly my pain, hurt, and sadness turned to anger and rage. This caused me to confront my mom. I began to yell at her. "Why would you do this? Dad has done so much for our family. He provides for us; he loves us; he cares for us; and has never hurt you or any of us kids!" I continued to yell at her as she sat there sobbing. Through my pain, I was relentless since there was nothing I could think of that would justify her actions.

With tears in her eyes, my mom began to fire back at me. She started rattling off things *not* to do when I get married. She yelled: "Don't take work calls when you're on a date with your wife!" "Don't neglect things your future wife needs you to do even if you think what she's asking you to do is not important!" "Always put her before others and make her a priority!"

I yelled back. "Even if dad did all those things, it still does not justify what you did!" The following few minutes were filled with back and forth yelling, leaving us both in tears. This was the darkest time of my life.

Things calmed down a bit, and my mom tried to hug me. For the first time in my life, I didn't want to be around her. I walked away as I rejected her hug.

I was beyond confused. I was angry, sad, hurt, and left feeling uncertain about what was going to happen with our family. I couldn't stop thinking about how much pain my dad was in, which made me hurt all the more. I needed all the pain to go away. I sat on the edge of my bed crying while listening to my mom sob downstairs.

The hurt was so extreme I actually had the thought of getting some drugs so I could simply numb-out. Instinctively, I knew that it was not the right thing to do, as well as I needed something long-lasting and not a temporary fix. I looked into the corner of my room and saw my guitar. I remembered times when my parents have

CHAPTER 10: KALEB, JOSHUA, JARED, AND FAITH

modeled for us kids and shared with us how important it is to turn to God when life is complicated. Well, this was one of those times.

I picked up my guitar and prayed for God to step into our mess and start working in our aching hearts. I played and sang at least a dozen worship songs. With tears running down my face, for the first time, I found myself crying out to the Lord. I asked Him to bring peace, healing, and His presence into our situation.

As I sang, the promise of Philippians 4:7, "And the peace of God, which transcends all understanding, will guard your hearts and your minds in Christ Jesus," flooded my soul. I learned that day that there is something supernatural about the presence of God. God's presence changes people, and it was changing me.

That evening I discovered that the authentic, sustainable peace people crave can only be found in Jesus. If I had chosen differently and medicated my emotions through a drug or alcohol, I wouldn't have found a divine peace, but rather a superficial peace, which in the end would have left me in pain and feeling empty.

Just a couple months after my mom's affair came out, a friend of mine came home to her dad who had just found out his wife was cheating on him. The way he handled it was by drinking, and his daughter immediately followed suit. After the alcohol wore off, she was back to where she had started emotionally, distraught and with zero peace. Watching her helped me realize I made the right choice that evening.

The next few days after finding out about my mom's sin were tough. I felt completely disconnected from her. Whenever I had a problem, or I needed to get something off my chest, I went to her for help. This time, when I needed my mom the most, I couldn't go to her because she was the one who had hurt me.

My silence didn't last long, and I was able to talk to her, give her the hug she wanted, and tell her I loved her. After a few weeks the words "I forgive you" were able to come out of my mouth with true authentic meaning behind them. I quickly learned that my forgiveness was not a one-time gift to our relationship, but a gift that I had to be willing to extend almost daily. I had to learn what Jesus meant in Matthew 18 when He told Peter not to forgive someone seven times, but instead 70 times seven. Some translations say 77 times. (My translation: do not keep track of wrongs and be willing to forgive an infinite amount.)

Offering my mom ongoing forgiveness was difficult because every time I remembered what had happened, it compromised my mood. No matter where I was in class, at school, at work, at the gym, at the skate park, or just driving around in my car, it would completely drain me of all joy. It was in those moments I had to re-forgive my mom and ask the Lord to help me to do so.

It took a few months to begin trusting my mom. Seeing my dad's willingness to trust her and give her a second chance helped me get to that same place. Seeing her leave her cell phone lying around made me feel she was not hiding anything. She allowed me access to her phone or iPad if I ever wanted to check up on her. Watching her and my dad do the tough work to rebuild their relationship produced inner confidence that she was getting better, which allowed my trust in her to grow.

When I look back on everything, I am incredibly grateful. I feel really good about my parents' relationship, and I know they are more in love with each other now than they ever have been. Their way of handling this situation has taught me so much. If it wasn't for Jesus, I don't believe my parents would be together today. I have learned that God is big enough to fix anything!

Today, I can say that I have forgiven my mom, and our relationship is stronger than ever; I love her so much. I still am and will always be a momma's boy. Also, it was important for me

CHAPTER 10: KALEB, JOSHUA, JARED, AND FAITH

to forgive my dad as well. Even though his actions did not justify my mom's affair, I did see the areas where he had failed as a husband, and at times as a father. I have learned a lot of what to do from my dad, as well as what not to do. My relationship with both my parents is great. I love them so much, and I could not be more proud; I could not ask for a better mom and dad!

JARED: I remember when my dad told me about my mom's affair. I was in my room watching Netflix on my Xbox. He came in and asked if I could pause my show. He sat down and shared that my mom and Chad had been having an affair. I was shocked. I remember thinking, "Wow, this is something you see in a movie." I never thought it could happen to our family. It took me a while to wrap my head around what she had done. It took some time for my mom's sin to sink in. It felt unreal. Living in a Christian home and my dad being a pastor, I never dreamed that adultery would be a part of my family's story.

Right after hearing the news, I was more confused than I was angry. I didn't understand why she did what she did. I didn't see it as only a betrayal between mom and my dad, but unfaithfulness to our entire family. I felt like she had cheated on me. It seemed as if the last few years before this were not real. Was she being fake to all of us? At the time of processing all this bad news, I wondered if my relationship with my mom was not enough for her and she had to do what she did. Thinking that broke my heart.

The worst part of this experience was not just knowing my mom had an affair, but there was the ongoing heartache it created in me as time went on. I remember being in my third-period weight-training class. Out of the blue, the thought of what my mom had done and what our family was going through hit me. Suddenly, I couldn't focus anymore. I became sad and angry. I lost all motivation to work out. My friends wondered why I stopped. I made up some excuse because I did not want to tell them the real reason.

There were times when we took a family trip down south and had to pass through the town where Chad lived. I'd put my earphones in and turn the music on and zone out, hoping to miss driving through his city on the freeway. Having to do that produced a sick feeling inside of me.

When it came to interacting with my mom, even though I was mad and hurt that she had messed up, there was something inside of me that made me feel a deep love for her. It was like I was sad for her. I assumed that when everything came out, all hell broke loose between her and my dad and Joshua since he was at home.

I remember having the thought to not add to what was already an emotional and tense situation but to simply love her. For me, not speaking for my siblings, it was important to make sure my mom knew I loved her, even though I was mad about what had happened. I felt my mom needed more hugs than anger coming at her.

I wanted my mom to change, but I was 15 years old and didn't know how I could even help with that. At the time, the only thing that made sense was to show her love and support. I figured if she was getting love from me it might make her recovery easier and set her up for success.

As time went on, I noticed my mom doing her devotions, which made me feel like she was making progress. I'd catch her singing worship songs around the house. Those times gave me confidence that things were getting better. I felt, and still do, that

CHAPTER 10: KALEB, JOSHUA, JARED, AND FAITH

if someone is walking closely with the Lord, they are in a better position to *not* fall morally the way my mom did.

A few years have gone by, and I don't tend to think about what happened. When it does come to mind or in conversation, I don't get mad anymore. I still recognize the situation was terrible, but because of where our family is today, my anger has been replaced with happiness and gratefulness. I am blown away by what God has done. He brought my parents back together. Their relationship is not perfect, but it is healthier. Our family pulled through a very dark time because of the Lord. For that reason, I don't dwell on the past but rather live and celebrate the present.

My encouragement to other kids who go through this is to talk out your feelings. Do your best not to hold everything inside. Find someone you trust, even a counselor, to help you sort out your feelings. What you're going through is traumatic, and you will need help. The more honest you are with how you feel, the healthier you will become. If you believe in God, then lean on Him. If you don't believe in the Lord, I encourage you to invite Him into your situation.

I can only speak for what happened in my family. All of us sprinted toward the Lord, clinging to Him as our only source of hope. He did a miracle and brought healing to all of us, healing that we are still walking out today.

FAITH: When I was 11 years old, I remember my dad telling me about my mom and Chad. My mom was outside playing with our dog, Scotch, and I was sitting at the island in our kitchen. My dad came in and told me he had to talk with me. At first, I thought I was going to get in trouble for something I didn't do or hear another lecture about how boys are gross and to stay away from them.

My dad told me that my mom had had an inappropriate relationship with Chad for the last few years. I was confused, because I wasn't sure what he meant by "inappropriate," although I had a hunch. I asked my dad if he was mad at my mom. He said, "Of course, but we're going to try to work it out by going to counseling."

After overhearing conversations between my brothers over the following days and weeks, I started to understand the magnitude of what my mom did. The more I came to learn, the more surreal it was for me. At 11 years of age, I felt numb emotionally, even when I was at school or hanging out with my friends. Sometimes I felt like I was lost in my own world; it was unbelievable to me that my mom had cheated on my dad.

My parents said they were going to work things out, and they were going to go to counseling, but I was also watching some of my friends' parents get divorced. I began to question if my parents would make it. Especially at night when going to bed, I often wondered all the *what-ifs* a kid might think of. *What if* it didn't work out between them? *What if* they got divorced? *What if* I'm forced to choose who to live with? *What if* my brothers and I got separated? This was the beginning of me battling depression.

I didn't know how to feel about my mom or how to act toward her. Should I be mad at her? Is it okay for me to be angry? I ended up basing my reaction on how my brothers handled our situation. They seemed to be nice and forgiving, so I decided that is what I had to do.

Looking back on that time, I understand that I shouldn't have followed their lead, but instead expressed my own feelings to my mom. I kept everything inside. I thought it was the quickest way to get things back to normal. If we didn't talk about it, we could just move on. Because I didn't express myself to my parents, I

CHAPTER 10: KALEB, JOSHUA, JARED, AND FAITH

got used to not sharing my feelings in general. I learned how to stuff them down inside, something today both my parents are constantly encouraging me not to do. I'm learning that most of the time not talking about things isn't the best way to go about solving a problem.

Shortly after learning about what my mom had done, I started to believe the affair could have been my fault. I thought that maybe I was not a good enough daughter, or maybe I didn't love my mom enough. Or because I'm stubborn and strong-willed and we argued, maybe I made her so mad that she wanted to be someone else's mom—like be a mother to Chad and Lauren's kids. The way I saw it was that if someone is acting stubborn and strong-willed toward me, it makes me really mad, so I don't want to be around them. I figured my mom felt the same way with me.

Not talking about how I felt, or what I was thinking, allowed me to believe that I may have caused the affair. Because of this, I began to battle depression. I found myself struggling with anxiety. Sometimes I'd overthink everything. My depression and anxiety caused tension between my parents and me.

If I got in trouble and was told I had misbehaved, I'd bring up my mom's past sin as a way of a comeback—something like, "Okay, I was bad and being grounded is my punishment, but you (mom) were bad too, what's your punishment?" That never went over well. Looking back on those moments, I realize I was being bratty and mean.

One of the things my parents did was be very open to all of us kids about the affair. They did not want it to become some bad secret that we all kept. Instead, they wanted it to be a topic that was okay to bring up, with the goal of flushing out our feelings.

However, because I never told anyone that I believed I was possibly the one to blame for our mom's actions, the topic was like nails on a chalkboard. I hated it whenever the subject came up. It just reminded me of what I thought I had caused. This is another reason to not keep things inside. I probably would have handled those conversations differently had it not been painful listening to them.

Just this last year, I have come to understand it was not my fault that my mom had an affair. My parents got me into counseling, and through various conversations, I began to piece together that it was my mom's decision and had nothing to do with me. I wish I had figured this out sooner.

If I had to give advice to someone, I'd tell them to write their feelings down and share them with someone they trust. I would tell them to try not to keep things inside because they might have the wrong idea about their situation, which may cause unnecessary pain.

Today, I am happy to say that my mom and I are continuing to work on our relationship. I have forgiven her and will work on continuing to forgive her. I love my mom (and dad) and I see us being close. To be honest, I still have a lot of work to do on myself. I need to work on being willing to share my feelings, even though it is difficult for me. I need to learn to listen more, and I need to learn when to keep quiet and not be so stubborn.

HEART CHECK

*All your children **shall** be taught by the Lord,
and great **shall** be the peace of your children.*
ISAIAH 54:13 (NKJV)

// 1. How have you created a *safe place* for your children to be who they are while learning and growing into responsible human beings?

_____
_____
_____
_____
_____
_____
_____
_____

// 2. Do you allow your children to share their *true* feelings regarding:

- Their life? _____
- You? _____
- Their problems? _____

// 3. How do you respond to your children when they are sharing their feelings?

_____
_____
_____
_____

// 4. Do your children ever witness you owning your mistakes? If so, please explain a time this happened.

_____
_____
_____
_____

// 5. Describe your "family time" with your children.

_____
_____
_____
_____

// 6. What does fun look like for you and your children?

_____
_____
_____
_____

CHAPTER 11

TIFFANY'S THOUGHTS
LEARNING FORGIVENESS, LIVING FORGIVEN

What a journey Rick and I have been—and still are—on. This experience has taught me so much. I wanted to take a moment and speak from my brokenness, as well as from a position of someone who is still in the process of being healed. I want to share a few things I have learned that shaped my thinking as I move forward in my relationship with the Lord and my marriage with Rick.

I feel I have a greater understanding of what it means to be forgiven. However, accepting forgiveness was very difficult for me because of the guilt I felt. When Rick came home that evening after staying at Eric's house the night he found out about my affair, he sat in front of me and told me he forgave me. I was hit with a wave of confusion. I could not comprehend why he would say that. I have heard the words "I forgive you" before. Most people have, but to hear them from Rick after I had done something so horrific to him and our family was mind-boggling; I felt so undeserving.

For the first time in my life, I experienced a new depth of love from God through Rick's forgiveness. I was brought back to the message of the cross. Jesus died for every sin I would ever commit, regardless of its impact on me and/or others. I was in awe when I realized that in addition to Jesus' forgiveness, which I did not deserve, God worked in Rick's heart to forgive me—again, when I did not deserve it. This was astounding to me! The Lord loved me enough to demonstrate His forgiveness through Christ, and He continued to love me by saving my marriage through the forgiveness of my husband.

I genuinely discovered how good it is to serve a loving and forgiving heavenly Father. Because of His love, grace, and mercy, He does not hold things against us. Micah 7:18 says, "Who is a God like you, who pardons sin and forgives the transgression of the remnant of his inheritance? You do not stay angry forever but delight to show mercy."

This mercy God delights in giving His children who confess their sin was something that became real in my life. When I saw the pain on the face of my loved ones because of a sin I committed against them, and they still forgave me, it was another example of God's love and compassion toward me.

Once I started to experience the miraculous forgiveness of God through Rick and our children, I began to forgive myself. Forgiving myself did not mean that I was going to forget what happened. I could not; nobody could. Experiencing their grace meant they were choosing to not hold on to what I had done, but instead they desired to move forward through healing.

Forgiving myself meant I started to follow suit. If God and my family wanted to move on, I decided maybe I should too. I slowly began to extend grace and mercy to *myself* and let go of my sin. I knew if I didn't, I would be allowing it to define me as a person, and it would be like an anchor holding me down. Because this is not easy to do, Dr. Ted and Diane were vital in helping me achieve self-forgiveness.

CHAPTER 11: TIFFANY'S THOUGHTS

This led me down the path of learning to not walk in shame. This was very difficult. Everywhere I went—church, my kids' school, the grocery store, my daughter's basketball games—I wanted to walk with my head down. I didn't want to look people in the eye.

Dr. Ted would continually told me, "Stop kissing shame. Remember, when you kiss shame, it's like kissing a rattlesnake. You'll get bit every time." Rick would often tell me to try to walk forgiven because I was.

Another place where I learned to not walk in shame was in my support group that Pure Desire Ministries connected me to. I met weekly with women who had committed the same sin I had. What I appreciated most about meeting with these ladies was that this was a safe place for me. I realized I was not alone, which defeated the enemy who loves to make people feel they are the only one who has failed in their area of transgression.

We are called to recognize that we are sinners in need of a Savior, but that does not mean we are to carry our sin around like baggage. Unfortunately, it was easy for me to want to hold onto the shame of my affair like carry-on luggage wherever I went. From time to time, I would forget Romans 8:1: "Therefore, there is now no condemnation for those who are in Christ Jesus." When I was reminded of this verse, it would help me to not carry my guilt, shame, and the burden of my sin. I learned that the enemy wanted me to be weighed down by my past behavior.

The two people who love me most—Jesus, my Savior, and Rick, my husband—had forgiven me. This gave me inner confidence to live and work on functioning as a forgiven individual. I began to walk with my head high. I remind myself often that I'm a child of God. I'm the apple of His eye. He loves me and has forgiven me. And, because my husband and children do as well, that's what ultimately matters. These truths allow me to walk confidently as a broken woman in the midst of being healed and *mended* by the Lord.

The enemy tempts me to kiss shame when I have to deal with a judgmental person. I understand what I did was wrong. When someone judged me, it was difficult not to get sucked into destructive thinking, like: "Yeah, I'm a bad person. I'm a wreck, I'm horrible."

Some people have said they forgave me but said they weren't sure they could still have a friendship with me due to *their* hurt. That was very sad to me, but I had to come to the point of realization that all I can do is apologize. If people can't be friends with me, I just have to be at peace, knowing it is potentially their issue and is something they have to sort out on their own with the Lord. I have to be okay with the various reactions people have— and ultimately leave it in God's hands.

Rick told me the Lord spoke to him and said that if we provided willing hearts to walk through the reconciling process, He would provide a miracle. As he and I accepted God's challenge, the miracle we came to understand was not singular but plural. It would be many miracles that would make up the overall miracle of restoration in our marriage and family. I began to not see forgiveness as just an act of pardoning someone for something they did wrong, but rather a supernatural miracle that God would use *through* people to minister *to* people for healing and restoration.

When we moved to pastor our church, God placed us directly across the street from Misael and Tawnya. We didn't know at the time that it was not an accident but by divine *placement*. Over the years, we became close with their family. Tawnya and I hung out all the time. It was common for her to walk across the street and

CHAPTER 11: TIFFANY'S THOUGHTS

just walk right in our front door and vice versa. While I was *living in sin*, living a *double life*, the woman that God placed across the street from us, when everything came out, never wavered in her love and care for me.

Two days after Rick found out about the affair, he went over to Misael and Tawnya's to share what happened. We both agreed we needed their support. This was the beginning of letting others know what had taken place in our family. As difficult as this was for me, I knew deep down inside that being vulnerable and inviting trusted friends into my mess was one of the first steps in getting healed.

Rick told me he cried hard in front of them as he broke the news. They both got up from their couch and hugged him and prayed with him. Then Tawnya, full of Christ-like compassion, walked across the street while Rick stayed with Misael.

I was in my bedroom, and I could not talk to anyone. I remember she came and sat on my bed and just held me while I sobbed. She told me she loved me and began to speak encouraging words. Tawnya assured me they were there for us and would not allow us to walk through this difficult time alone. Her heart for me was another example of God's miraculous forgiveness even though I had been living in sin. We continued to get together as the days, weeks, and months, and even years, went on. She was always right there with her arm around me. She loved on me, and I am forever grateful for our friendship.

In addition to Tawnya, God had other people continually reach out to me—like Margaret and her weekly letters with encouraging words. My good friend Judy texted and called me frequently while we were away from our church to heal. She always told me that she loved me. She reminded me that nobody is without sin and we all need grace.

Every time someone said they loved me, it was like I felt their hand on my back supporting me. Over time, it felt like I had hands up and down my spine because of the amount of support I received from others. This gave me the strength to carry on in recovery and not walk in shame.

Experiencing moments of acceptance gave me the strength to walk with my head high. The more love and forgiveness I felt from others, the more comforted I felt by the Lord. The Bible is filled with references to God being our Comforter. In Jeremiah 8:18 it says, "You who are my Comforter in sorrow." God is the God of all comfort, and that is the very sensation I felt as He sent people my way to love on me. I greatly enjoyed His comfort versus carrying the weight of my sin.

One of the heaviest things I have ever had to carry in my life was my secret sin. It crushed me emotionally. It was exhausting having to live two separate lives. I got tired of hiding and looking over my shoulder while putting on a façade. The weight of my sin was never intended for me to carry.

I can only imagine the immense pressure Jesus felt carrying the sins of the world. The Old Testament prophet, Isaiah said that He bore the sin of many. He bore my sin, your sin, the world's sin—past, present, and future. And, He had never even experienced sin in any way. I was being crushed under the weight of *just* my sin alone; I can't imagine what Jesus felt when the sin of the entire world was placed on Him.

Christ knows what it feels like to carry the burden of sin. He can relate to the heaviness it brings on someone. If you've ever carried unconfessed sin, all bottled-up inside, you might know what I'm talking about. With the Lord, there is no weight of condemnation for past sin. It is a burden that is lifted. Something Rick and I quoted a lot during counseling was 1 John 1:9, "If we

CHAPTER 11: TIFFANY'S THOUGHTS

confess our sins, he is faithful and just and will forgive us our sins and purify us from all unrighteousness." This confession—this acknowledgment of our wrongdoings—purifies us as if we never committed the offense. When we accept and walk in forgiveness, it can remove the weight of our iniquity.

Before people can be freed from the burden of their sin, they must own it. They must take responsibility for their actions. It's too easy to fall into the trap of blaming others for our poor decisions. Saying, or even worse, believing that Rick made me have an affair is ridiculous. He did not make me do anything. I chose to do what I did, to cope by engaging in an immoral relationship. If I blamed him, I would not be feeling the full weight (seriousness) of my sin because I would have shifted the burden onto him. If I'm not feeling the true weightiness of my transgression, I will be less repentant—if at all. If you own your sin, you know how heavy it is; you'll feel the weight of it.

Sin drives a person. It will either turn you to the Lord or away from Him. If it pushes you toward God and you confess and own your wrongdoing, you position yourself to receive healing from the Lord. James 5:16: "Confess your sins to each other…so that you may be healed." Confession is the first step in getting healed. However, if you do not own your sin, you will not be restored and, therefore, you run the risk of repeating the behavior and causing more pain to yourself and others.

With that said, confession is not easy. It can be brutal. Disclosing that you're having an affair, or any other sin that will send a shockwave through your family and/or circle of friends, is scary. When there is so much to lose, you can be frozen in fear and just do nothing. When you have something to share with the magnitude to alter your life drastically, one is *not* typically quick to engage. Preparing yourself to tell someone—your spouse specifically—is like knowing that in 10 minutes you have to flip a switch in an airplane that will cause it to crash. There is no smooth landing.

The impact and destruction of the news are going to take your breath away. You will get dizzy. You will not be able to see straight. You will not be able to breathe. Once you flip the switch, there's no turning back, and you know you're going down. This knowledge of what will happen is what keeps you from flipping the switch and coming clean sooner.

It is in these moments that you're caught in the ultimate double bind: a lose/lose situation.[10] If you don't bring your sin out from hiding, it will continue to eat at you and destroy you emotionally. But if you flip the switch, the plane will go down, and there will be pain involved, and no guarantee of recovery.

This is why it takes so long for people to confess. Sometimes you run out of time, and the plane flies into the side of a mountain, and you get caught before you admit your hidden secret. Now, you have a whole other hurdle to jump over if you're going to try to redeem the now-damaged relationship. My encouragement to anyone who has a hidden sinful secret is to come clean. Tell a trusted friend what you're doing. Unburden yourself from the very sin that has trapped you.

For three years, I was held captive to a secret. So many times I wanted the truth to be known because the weight of my sin was crushing me, ruining my marriage, and distancing me from my children. There were times I came so close to telling my mom the sinful state I had allowed myself to get ensnared in, but I froze every time. As much as I wanted to, revealing my deep dark secret that would send my life into a tailspin without the promise of

---

10. Ibid. 57.

CHAPTER 11: TIFFANY'S THOUGHTS

recovery immobilized me—something the enemy worked hard at, which kept me emotionally imprisoned. Regardless, if you got caught or if you flipped the switch and dealt with your sin head-on, if counseling is available, take advantage of it. Counseling will not be a picnic. It could make you angry, sad, and frustrated. It may even be gut-wrenching at times.

Not to be gross, but people will typically enter into counseling with emotional wounds that have scabbed over but were never really healed. The counselor, if they're good at what they do, will lovingly start to pick at the scabbed areas. It will cause discomfort, but hopefully, at some point, the scab will open, and pus will begin to come out. It's messy and difficult, but it is the very thing you need. The counselor will dress your wound now that the infection is no longer hidden. It is exposed and removed from the scabbed area. With newly provided wisdom and a go-forward plan, the healing begins.

Counseling can provide you with insight that radically changes your opinion or view of how you saw things before. Some of this may make you feel good, but sometimes it is a sobering reality check that feels like you got punched in the stomach.

Through our conversations with Dr. Ted and Diane, my eyes were opened to many things. I was challenged about how to respond to specific situations that I had yet to experience. They were good at forecasting what Rick and I were about to encounter through our healing process because they had walked this road with many other couples.

Counseling helped me see that I had emotionally separated myself from my family when I was living in sin. My focus was not on them, but rather on medicating myself with a sinful relationship.

Sin has the power to make you selfish. I was not caring for my family as I should have. I did not love on my children the way the Lord wanted me to. I distanced myself from Rick. My sin made me crabby, angry, tired, and numb. I began to drink too much wine at night because I could not believe what I was doing. My duplicity was the most selfish thing I have ever done. Counseling made me face this hard truth.

The treatment and counseling we received from Pure Desire Ministries taught me that accountability was the fastest way to build trust with Rick and our kids. And, there was a safety plan in place that had consequences if I relapsed. If there was any contact with Chad initiated by either of us, and Rick was not informed, it would equal one month of me living at my parents, who live almost three hours away from my family. I am happy to say there has been zero contact and we never had to do that.

I learned that the road to regaining trust was going to be long and bumpy. Rick had password access to everything of mine: email account, cell phone—all social media accounts—when I got back on them. I left my phone lying around instead of keeping it on me at all times. Rick could check anything at any time. I decided early on to be patient with this part of our recovery process.

After a year or two into recovery, Rick checked on me. It took me by surprise because I thought he'd been doing okay and trust had been rebuilt. I had to work on not being defensive and remind myself that the road is *long and bumpy*. Those were sobering moments.

Dr. Ted and Diane helped me see that my sin had a ripple effect; it was not just between God and me or Rick and me. My sin affected our kids, all of our friends and family, our church, and even the church we came from that Lauren and Chad were part of.

Sin rarely affects just one individual. It often drags the innocent through the mud as well. I solely blame myself for

CHAPTER 11: TIFFANY'S THOUGHTS

my affair. It was my choice. I should not have done it. To cope and get rid of my pain, I could have spoken to my mom, gotten counseling for myself, or insisted that Rick and I get counseling. But I did not. If I wanted to receive healing and have the best chance of real recovery with Rick and our family, owning my sin and getting outside help was the best option.

Today, as I write this, I am counting my blessings. I am grateful for God's never-ending forgiveness, mercy, and grace. I feel loved like never before. I'm thankful for my new relationship with Rick and the love and forgiveness my children have extended to me. I am grateful for the loving support of my parents. Their kindness and compassion toward me, along with that from my siblings, make walking through recovery with Rick easier.

God is truly a *God of second chances*. He has given Rick and me a fresh start, for which I am so happy. I sit here astonished at the miracles we have experienced over the last few years. Jesus has kept His promise! My marriage and family surviving has humbled me greatly. But as if that were not enough, God pulled off another miracle—one that some people celebrate and some don't know how to feel about it because it is unnatural.

Lauren was not ready to forgive me for a long time, which I understood. I was her friend and had an affair with her husband. I reached out to her about a year or so after everything came out, but she was not ready to talk. I knew I needed to give her space, as well as come to grips that our friendship was over. While I was having my affair, I consciously thought about all the pain it was going to cause her. It killed me that my selfish behavior was hurting the ones I loved, including Lauren. I was worried about what it was going to do to her. I always thought about how I was betraying her. Lauren was kind, loving, and generous. We had so much fun together. Like Rick and our kids, she and her children did not deserve this. In my broken, sinful state, I selfishly medicated at her expense.

About two years after I reached out to Lauren, who was not yet ready to talk, I received a text from her. It said, "I know it's been awhile, but I am ready to talk if you still are?" I was shocked. This text was out of the blue. I was nervous but eager to get together with her. I told her I was still willing to meet. A few days later, we met up for dinner at a local restaurant.

Lauren was warm and friendly; she was different than I had anticipated. She had an inner peace that served as strength. We talked for hours extending heartfelt words and simply catching up. A few days later, I received a text from Lauren thanking me for our time together. To be extended forgiveness from the very woman I betrayed humbled me greatly. God is good!

HEART CHECK

If we confess our sins, he is faithful and just and will forgive us our sins and purify us from all unrighteousness.

I JOHN 1:9

// **1. Forgiveness is a decision; it is a choice. Is there someone or a situation God is asking you to forgive?**

_____
_____

By God's grace, I *decide* to forgive _____
for _____.

// **2. Forgiveness is emotional. As healing happens emotionally, it becomes easier to take this step. Have you been emotionally healed? If yes, briefly describe. If no, who could help you take this next step?**

_____
_____
_____
_____
_____

// **3. Reflect on Jesus' forgiveness and thank Him.**
Rewrite Colossians 3:12–13 by inserting your name in first blank and your offender's name in the remaining two blanks:

Since God chose (me) to be the holy people He loves, _____ clothe yourself with tenderhearted mercy, kindness, humility, gentleness, and patience. Make allowance for _____ faults, and forgive _____ who offended (me). Remember, the Lord forgave (me), so I must forgive others.

// **4. Have you forgiven yourself for past mistakes?**
☐ Yes ☐ No

Do you feel revenge, anger, judgment, or self-denial? Seek release not relief.

_____
_____
_____
_____
_____

Have you learned why you committed the offense?

_____
_____
_____
_____
_____

Do you feel shame for the offense or sorrow for those you offended? "Sorrow" will help move you past the "shame."

___

Is there something you can do to right the wrong? If not, can you trust God to take care of it?

___

// 5. **If you have forgiven yourself, how has it changed your life?**

___

CHAPTER 12

RICK'S THOUGHTS
A CAUTIONARY TALE

It is 5:34 a.m. as I sit here in our home writing my final thoughts. I'm thinking about all that I have gone through post-affair. I'm blown away by the grace and mercy of my King Jesus! I often think back on the day He whispered to me, "You provide the heart; I'll provide the miracle." He was not joking! He has and continues to live up to His side of the bargain, even when I've wanted to give up.

Journeying to reconciliation and restoring our family was not an easy road to travel. It has been the hardest thing I've ever chosen to do, but also, the most rewarding. I feel like I had an *emotional* version of what the Apostle Paul (then Saul) experienced in his second encounter with Jesus in Acts 9. He's on the road to Damascus *doing what he wanted to do* when suddenly he found himself in an unscheduled meeting with Jesus (first encounter), which left him physically blind for three days.

Then a gentleman by the name of Ananias showed up at the house Paul had been led to by his friends, and he prayed for him. Acts 9:17, "Then Ananias went to the house and entered it. Placing his hands on Saul, he said, 'Brother Saul, the Lord—

Jesus, who appeared to you on the road as you were coming here—has sent me so that you may see again and be filled with the Holy Spirit'" (second encounter). At that point, something like scales fell from his eyes, and he could see again.

Paul's physical and spiritual healing experience not only restored his natural sight, but also his past and future perspective on life. He saw clearly the way he was living and the way he needed to live moving forward. With new lenses to view life through, Saul (turned Paul) was a changed man.

That's how I see my experience. I was cruising through life, doing what I wanted to do, married with four children, in ministry, and all of a sudden I'm having an unscheduled meeting with Jesus. I found out my wife of 20 years (at the time) was having a three-year-long affair right under my nose.

Then the Lord sent a few Ananiases my way (Dr. Ted and Diane Roberts, Don Smith, Eric Stevenson, Dan Driscoll, to name a few) that, at different times, all ministered to me. While always encouraging, they were brutally honest with their words. It was in those Ananias moments that scales fell from my eyes (figuratively speaking), and I began to see more clearly the actual condition of my marriage.

As time went on, my vision became clearer, and I became more disgusted with how I had failed to lead my family and Tiffany as Christ calls a man to lead.

I remember the first time I started to see things a little more clearly. Tiffany and I were on a road trip and stopped at a fast-food restaurant. When I got out of our car, I noticed the vehicle parked next to us. It was nasty! It was beat up on the outside and the paint was faded all over, seemingly losing a battle to the rust that was everywhere. The tires were bald, the windows dirty, and it sounded like a V6 running on four cylinders. It was pitiful. As I got out of our van, I took in the condition of this car in a matter of seconds. And then it was as if the Lord spoke to me and said, "That vehicle represents the true state of your marriage. But, you're on the inside driving and thinking you're in a beautiful car."

I was shocked at the imagery of this analogy. I mean, I knew our marriage was not perfect, but I thought it was at least good. I wouldn't have chosen *that car* as the visual aid to describe the condition of my relationship with Tiffany, but I had been blinded to this harsh reality. Tiffany and I always had a friendship. We could make each other laugh, and being intimate was never a problem as it was great and frequent. However, even though these things were true, our marriage was still very damaged and broken. I just couldn't see it; I couldn't see it until the Lord revealed it to me.

If I had a flux capacitor like Marty McFly did in the movie *Back to the Future*,[11] and I could go back in time, I'd visit little Ricky Bulman and have a heart-to-heart with him. Here are a few things I have learned through this whole ordeal that I would share with my younger self:

COMMIT TO KEEPING GOD FIRST IN THE RELATIONSHIP

We are called to keep the Lord in first position in our lives. Proverbs 3:6 says, "In *all* your ways submit to him." Proverbs 16:3 says, "*Commit* to the Lord whatever you do." Philippians 4:6 says, "Do not be anxious about anything, but in *every situation*, by prayer and petition, with thanksgiving, present your requests to God."

Scripturally, we are to acknowledge God in *all* of what we do in life. *This applies to a marriage relationship.* We are to *commit* our

---

11. Gale, B. (Producer), & Zemeckis, R. (Director). (1985). *Back to the Future* [Motion Picture]. USA: Universal Pictures.

actions to the Lord. *This applies to a marriage relationship.* We are to bring *every situation* to God—all our needs, wants, and desires. By the way, yes, *this applies to a marriage relationship.* Am I starting to sound like a broken record, little Ricky Bulman?

I heard this illustration many years ago, and it has always stuck with me. Placing God at the center of your life is like spokes converging into the hub of a bicycle tire. The hub is the centerpiece that provides all the strength, security, and function of the wheel. All the spokes are placed in the rim and strategically meet into the center hub. Everything connects into the hub of the wheel. Without a hub to bind to, the tire cannot work correctly. The rim is weakened.

The same is true with the Lord. If Jesus is not the center (*the hub*) of our lives (our work, our play, our friendships, our finances, our marriage, and family), then we've weakened it. Those things truly have nothing to fasten to. They exist but are not supported properly.

We are setting ourselves up for failure when God is not invited to be the center of all we do. It is pretty arrogant to think we can handle everything on our own. When God is at the core of all we do, the level of success is exponential.

As men, as husbands, lead your family this way. Invite God into your parenting plan. Invite Him to be a part of how you steward your money. Invite Him to be a part of your daily conversations, frequently incorporating Him as a topic of discussion. Pray with your spouse and kids *daily*. Pray together as a family. If it is awkward at first, push through it; the awkwardness will soon fade away. Doing life *without* Jesus is like trying to ride a bicycle with a tire that has the hub missing and spokes dangling wildly everywhere—it is *dysfunctional.*

CHAPTER 12: RICK'S THOUGHTS

LOVE YOUR WIFE AS CHRIST LOVED THE CHURCH

This was an area where I missed the boat big time, and I'm grateful the Lord has given me a second chance to do it right with Tiffany. Paul writes in Ephesians 5:25, "Husbands, love your wives, just as Christ loved the church and gave himself up for her."

I remember Dr. Ted asking what I thought that verse meant. Before I could answer, he said, "It means you get to die first." I chuckled; I understood what he was getting at.

The word "love" here is a Greek word *agapao*, which is a type of love that seeks the best, the highest good for someone else. It is a completely *unselfish* type of love. It is the level of commitment and serving that Jesus modeled, which ultimately led to Him sacrificially give up His life by way of death on a cross.

What Paul instructed husbands to do is live selflessly. Die to yourself daily and serve your wife. This requires a commitment to sacrificial actions that benefit your spouse. As husbands we *should be* approaching every day with the mentality, "What can I do to make today better for my wife; how can I serve her?" Notice that I italicized the words "should be." That is a nod in your direction, something I too "should" do.

It's not easy to do. We have wants and desires. And sometimes, we just don't want to make a sacrifice. However, it is when we have this attitude that we open the door to potential friction and conflict in the relationship.

Here's the good news. I found out that the more I intentionally serve Tiffany, it has an amazing effect on her. She suddenly starts serving me. She starts insisting I get what I want. In a weird way, it becomes a love fest, and everyone wins. I only mention this truth not so your motive is anything other than wanting to be obedient to God by loving your wife the way He called men to do, but rather to help you see there is a by-product of such obedience. Complying with God's directive to love your wife as Christ loved the church will give you a fulfilling marriage where you do not ultimately miss out. Trust me; it works!

KEEP THE TOP TWO PRIORITIES THE TOP TWO

As a Christian, making and keeping God priority number one is paramount. The question is, who or what will be number two? Scripturally, God is to be first. Deuteronomy 6:5 and Mark 12:30 tell us to "love the Lord your God with all your heart and with all your soul and with all your mind and with all your strength."

He is supposed to be our all-in-all, our *número uno*, our top priority, which places Him as the foundation we build all of life upon. When God is number one, then He is the bedrock that safely secures a marriage. To not make Jesus a priority is like living in a house without a foundation. It may work for a season, but it is not built to endure threatening storms: the stronger the foundation, the stronger the house. The same is true for marriage and life. With God as the foundation for *all* relationships and decisions, we have a better chance weathering anything that comes our way.

For a married couple, the marriage is next in line as a priority. *Not the kids*, not work, not the church, not our hobbies, but the relationship between a husband and his wife. In the beginning, when God established the marriage institution, notice what He instructed in Genesis 2:24, "Therefore shall a man leave his father and his mother, and *shall cleave unto his wife: and they shall be one flesh*."

This speaks to the utmost commitment next to our bond with God. *Cleave* and *one flesh* speak of the level of commitment a husband and wife must have toward one another. There needs

CHAPTER 12: RICK'S THOUGHTS

to be a covenantal bond established where new loyalties and new priorities are for each other.

Notice, dear little Ricky Bulman what it does *not* say, "And shall cleave unto his *career*; and they shall be one" or "and shall cleave unto his *hobbies*; and they shall be one" or "and shall cleave unto his *kids*; and they shall be one…"

No, it states that in a marriage relationship the "cleaving to" and the "becoming one" are solely between a husband and wife. When one of them begins to cleave to something or someone else, healthy jealousy can surface.

We typically think of jealousy negatively, but there is such a thing as good or healthy jealousy. Paul states in 2 Corinthians 11:2, "I am jealous for you with a *godly jealousy*." When we make the Lord second to anything, even He gets jealous. In Exodus 20:3, 5, God says, "You shall have no other gods before me…I, the Lord your God, am a *jealous God*."

We all have the potential for jealousy. When it comes to marriage, the same jealousy God has for us can exists in the hearts of a husband and wife. The jealousy, when it is godly and aligns with the rules and roles outlined in scripture, can protect the marriage. But like anything else, the enemy wants to pervert what God has intended for good and use jealousy to cause division: something to which we all need to be on guard.

As soon as the cleaving shifts from a spouse—to the career, the hobbies, the kids, the church, or money—a natural jealousy surfaces because the priority order God has laid out is out of balance. When this happens, the couple will turn their focus elsewhere, and the marriage has officially started to spiral ever so slowly downward. If not corrected immediately, the division between them will gain momentum and potentially lead them to a place they never wanted to be.

EDUCATE YOURSELF ABOUT YOUR SPOUSE

If I were speaking to my younger self, I'd share that one of the biggest mistakes Tiffany and I made was that we never considered understanding the relational dynamics we each had as we grew up in our families of origin. It was not even on our radar.

We knew we both had grown up in Christian homes and found out that we shared the same biblical values. We also went as far as to share our past sins and issues with each other. We sat down one evening and put it all out on the table for full disclosure; it was scary but good for us.

However, we never thought about trying to understand the relational dynamic we may have had with our parents—it never crossed our minds. Over the years, neither of us thought to ask about the rules we each lived under or the habits and traditions our family had that we liked or disliked.

I wish I could tell little Ricky Bulman to ask Tiffany about the things she admired about her father. I'd tell him to ask her if there were things she swore she would do differently when she got married. I would encourage him to inquire about various childhood experiences she had and how they made her feel.

I'd urge him to find out what the rules were in her household regarding cleaning her room or the kitchen, her chores, curfew, and dating. I would tell little Ricky to ask her what she thought was fair versus unfair.

These might seem like odd things to ask, but the answers would shed some light on what expectations she might have for the marriage and the family—expectations she might not even realize were there (*unspoken rules*).

Then I would tell my younger self to share my experiences so the two of us could at least have an awareness of why one

CHAPTER 12: RICK'S THOUGHTS

might be reacting or not reacting a certain way when there was an issue. Doing this would have saved Tiffany and me from many misunderstandings about our quality of care and love for each other, and many of our fights could have possibly been avoided.

Then, after little Ricky had heard everything Tiffany loved and appreciated about her dad, I'd tell him to do those things, even if he wouldn't have thought to do them on his own. The little girl that admired her father's actions will *naturally* be looking for that same quality of care in her husband. And, equally important, if there were things she did not like, try to avoid committing those actions as best as possible to prevent triggers.

As men, we are to care for and protect our wives, not just physically, but emotionally as well. Identifying her childhood admirations and dislikes can be used as a guide in how to conduct yourself with your wife. Proper premarital counseling is a must and can help flush out some of the expectations the engaged couple may have for each other and their future family.

LEARN EACH OTHER'S LOVE LANGUAGES

Tiffany and I did not know that each of us possessed "love languages" until after 17 years of being married. Once we read Gary Chapman's book, *The Five Love Languages: How to Express Heartfelt Commitment to Your Mate*, we found out what our top three love languages were, and we both had an epiphany. We were speaking our love language to the other person for our entire marriage and *not* speaking their love language. Here are our top three love languages:

- **Tiffany:** Acts of Service, Gifts, and Quality Time
- **Rick:** Words of Affirmation, Quality Time, and Physical Touch

We realized that each of us often spoke our love language to the other. When Tiffany brought me a Kit Kat candy bar from the store, I said thank you, but didn't get giddy about it like she did if I brought her something.

I told Tiffany every day she looked beautiful. She appreciated the comment and said thank you, but I always felt she didn't appreciate it as much as I did when she complimented me. It is just not her love language.

I could not walk by her without lovingly (not annoyingly) patting her butt or hip affectionately (nothing sexual). I did that because I like physical touch. She grew to find it endearing, but it was not an emotional need she sought to have filled.

Tiffany did kind things, "acts of service," specifically for me. She always seemed excited about what she did and wanted me to have that same level of delight. When I didn't (because it was not my love language), although I appreciated the gesture, it offended her.

When I emptied the dishwasher, you'd have thought I bought her a car based on her excitement. I'm thinking, "It's not that big of a deal; I'm just putting plates away." It was a huge deal because "acts of service" is her language. If I came home with flowers, she lit up as if it was Christmas. Why? Gifts are a language she speaks. Actually, I think all wives speak that language to some degree.

Part of the problem couples have in connecting emotionally with each other is that they are speaking the wrong love language to their spouse. Think about how effective it is if you speak Spanish to someone who speaks Italian. The languages are close but also different. You might have small success in communicating, but your frustration would grow quickly. Why? Because you're not speaking their language; you're speaking what you know—*your language*.

CHAPTER 12: RICK'S THOUGHTS

Married couples make this mistake with their love language communication all the time, and then wonder why they're not connecting emotionally with each other. Learning and communicating in your spouse's love languages will bring you closer together as you connect at a deeper level.

GET PERSONAL COUNSELING IMMEDIATELY

Getting counseling is not a sign of weakness but rather a sign of strength and maturity. It is an act of humility. It's someone admitting they need to talk through their feelings or situations to process them properly and achieve a preferred outcome. I wish I had done it. Even though I had loving parents and my childhood was good—not perfect, but not bad either—I still processed my experiences in such a way that it shaped my behavior. It shaped a lot of good in me, but also I came away from my upbringing with unresolved issues. We all have them to various degrees.

Some of my problems stemmed from not understanding what was happening in my life. As a child, my brain was cataloging experiences, while at the same time trying to make sense of everything. Along the way, I came to certain conclusions about life and myself in general that may or may not have been accurate or true.

Nonetheless, I took certain beliefs and behaviors into my marriage with Tiffany, and coupled with not knowing her very well, it was a recipe for disaster. Getting counseling could have helped me sort out many issues I was aware of and even those I wasn't aware of. Personal counseling would not have safeguarded me 100 percent from the pitfalls of my marriage, but it would have increased my percentage of having a healthier and better relationship with Tiffany.

Our third son Jared, at 19 years of age, came to me and said, "Dad, I want to get counseling." I was shocked! He desired this all on his own. Thinking it was probably a good idea, I asked him why. He said, "I know I have issues and I know I have issues I'm not aware of. Doesn't it make sense for me to go to counseling and work on myself while I'm single before I find my wife and get married?"

My jaw hit the floor! Such wisdom coming from my baby boy blew me away. I praised him for the way he was thinking. I told him I wished I had done that.

He said, "Please don't be offended, but watching you and mom go through everything just made me think if I get counseling now, maybe I wouldn't bring as much garbage into the marriage and therefore avoid what we all went through."

I just smiled at him and told him I was proud of him for tracking this way. I wanted to kiss him, but he does not like me kissing his hairy face.

Think like Jared and get counseling. It will not solve all future problems, but it very well could set you up for greater success in your marriage. Think of it this way: getting to know yourself better will make you a better person and spouse.

I wish I could go back in time and share these six pearls of wisdom (and many more) to my younger self, but I can't. However, I am here today with an opportunity to do marriage right, as I spend the next 20, 30, or 40 years married to an amazing woman.

HEART CHECK

Love is patient, love is kind. It does not envy, it does not boast, it is not proud. It does not dishonor others, it is not self-seeking, it is not easily angered, it keeps no record of wrongs.

I CORINTHIANS 13:4–5

// 1. Describe your spouse's childhood. What events and actions made your spouse feel loved and cherished?

_____
_____
_____
_____
_____
_____

// 2. How do you meet your spouse's emotional needs based on what you know about your spouse's childhood?

_____
_____
_____
_____
_____

// 3. Do you have regular times of interaction discussing how you can enrich your marriage? Explain.

_____
_____
_____

// 4. How do you physically serve your spouse in everyday life?

_____
_____
_____

// 5. What is your spouse's love language? How do you reinforce that love language?

_____
_____
_____

// 6. Are you intentional with your marriage maintenance? If yes, who are your counselors and advocates for your marriage? Who are your accountability partners?

_____
_____
_____
_____

CHAPTER 13

EPILOGUE
A FRESH START

As we sit back and reflect on all the Lord has done and is *continuing* to do in our marriage and family, we are beyond humbled. It is incredible the miracles that take place when one surrenders pain and guilt to the Lord. When we lay our offenses at the feet of Jesus and say, "I surrender _____ to You. How do You want me to proceed?" and then obey what He says, you instantly become a candidate for a miracle. Letting go of control and placing it in God's hands, albeit not easy, is the smartest thing you can do for the best outcome you can hope for.

We've experienced the miracle of Romans 8:28: "And we know that in all things God works for the good of those who love him, who have been called according to his purpose." No matter what happens in our life, God is big enough to reconstruct our experiences into something good for us, which ultimately He can use to further His kingdom. He's the master at taking what the enemy meant for evil, turning the tables on him, and bringing something crazy-glorious back to Jesus.

That's precisely what the Lord did in our marriage. The enemy came to steal, kill, and destroy our relationship and family: but God stepped in and used what Satan did *against* him to reveal to us what needed to be fixed.

This horrific experience did not push us away from each other or away from the Lord, but instead drove us *closer* together and made us fall *more in love* with Jesus. Satan's plan backfired. What the enemy wove for evil, God re-wove for good. God is the master builder and that's what He did with us. He seized the opportunity of our horrible situation and used it to rebuild our marriage.

This happened to Joseph in the Old Testament. He was sold into slavery by his older brothers. Twenty-plus years later he sees them again. Genesis 50:20 records Joseph telling them, "...you meant evil against me, *but* God meant it for good in order to *bring about* this present result, to preserve many people alive" (NASB).

In Hebrew, the phrase to "bring about" means to produce, to prepare, carrying the idea of a builder. This verse basically tells us that God is mighty enough to take the wreckage of our tough circumstances and build a masterpiece out of it that brings Him the most glory and helps fulfill His purpose for our lives.

The picture of our marriage today is drastically different from before the affair. We see it as an "imperfect beauty." We have a beautiful relationship, but it is definitely imperfect. We still have gray cloudy days, with occasional storms. However, our approach to how we handle the storms is different. Now, we have tools to help us navigate through those times, without causing damage to our relationship. Do we sometimes mess up and have to eat crow? Yes! This go-round we have a greater awareness of each other's wiring and how to communicate for the best result. We are learning to continuously extend grace to one another.

CHAPTER 13: EPILOGUE

RICK: I am dialed into Tiffany's love languages. I continually work on speaking *her* language to her instead of my language. I am dialed in a lot more concerning my insecurities and how they led to behavior that damaged Tiffany.

I'm daily working on serving my wife and loving her as Christ loved the church. This requires me to consciously keep my selfishness in check. I'm always coaching myself and checking my motives. When I fail, I do my best to own it and ask Tiffany for forgiveness.

And, yes, I lock up the house and make sure we are all secured inside. In fact, when I catch Tiffany doing it out of habit, I quickly tell her, "Honey, I've got it. I'll lock up. Please let me do this." We are creating new habits where I'm doing more of the things she used to do on my behalf.

As for Chad, it has taken me about four and half years to forgive him. Forgiving him does not mean he is off the hook and all is okay between us. Forgiveness does not automatically mean reconciliation; a reuniting of the friendship.

Forgiveness is foundationally between God and me. It is me choosing to release Chad to the Lord and not holding his wrong over him, not excusing his wrong, but deciding to not put any more energy into chaining Chad to his past mistakes. I do not have the power to free him, and I do not have the authority to sentence him. *I'm not God.*

I cannot control Chad; I can only control my feelings toward him. I asked myself one day, "You have enough baggage to carry in your life, why would you want to add more by carrying the burden of resentment and unforgiveness toward a person you cannot change?"

I decided to free myself and hand him over to the Lord. I did so by sitting down and writing him a letter. It wasn't a long letter but communicated enough to let him know that I was no longer choosing to be angry and resentful toward him and that he is in the Lord's hands. I shared that my prayer for him is that he could reconcile his heart back to the Lord and work things out with Jesus. In doing so, I felt a freedom that only Jesus can give, and that is worth celebrating!

TIFFANY: I have noticed a significant change in our marriage. I'm crazy about my husband again. Although he's not perfect, he's making great strides in changing and being more responsive to the husbandly duties he used to neglect.

Now that I have a greater understanding of his wiring and why he tracked mentally the way he did for all those years, I find that my anger, disappointment, and feelings that caused me to question his love for me are gone.

I'm now able to connect the dots, which provides the grace I need to extend toward him. Through using the communicative tool, The Gottman Exercise[12] (see next chapter), he and I can flush out in an amicable way how the other made us feel.

I know that my anger has been a huge source of our fighting. I realized through counseling that I might have exasperated our issues, putting Rick and me into a tailspin. These days, I'm learning how to respond in a more controlled manner. While at times I fail, because of the grace Rick and the kids continually give me, I'm getting better at manifesting the self-control aspect of the fruit of the Spirit.

---

12. Schwartz Gottman, J. & Gottman, J. (2015). *10 Principles for Doing Effective Couples Therapy*. New York, NY: W. W. Norton & Company.

CHAPTER 13: EPILOGUE

RICK AND TIFFANY: We are proud to say that we all have, at some point, entered into individual counseling. We even put it in our monthly budget. Our kids are and have gone through personal counseling to help them walk through their pain and issues. They too did not escape the emotional trauma that Rick and Lauren felt. There is still residual emotional damage that raises its head from time to time. But, as a family, we are all committed to working and walking out this healing process together.

We now go to individual counseling rather than together. We love it! We are confident we still have blind spots that, if revealed, can make our marriage and us healthier. This *ongoing maintenance* is healthy and nothing to be ashamed of. We know we are like the marred clay in the potter's hand (Jeremiah 18:4). And through counseling, the Lord continues to mold our mentality to healthier thinking, which leads to improved actions and responses.

We want to leave you with this: your mistakes do not *diminish* your value. Romans 8:38–39 says, "For I am convinced that neither death nor life, neither angels nor demons, neither the present nor the future, nor any powers, neither height nor depth, nor anything else in all creation, will be able to separate us from the love of God that is in Christ Jesus our Lord." Translation: you can't be bad enough to make God stop loving you, and you can't be good enough to make Him love you more. Your sin does not cancel God's desire to heal, redeem, and use you for His glory.

Your mistakes may have caused a detour in your life—like they did in ours—but there is hope for you. Your sin is not bigger than God—it does not trump His ability to do good in your life. With the powerful working hand of God, coupled with your submissive heart, He can redeem anything and create an imperfect beauty in you.

OUR FAMILY...
HEALTHY, BUT IMPERFECTLY BEAUTIFUL!

CHAPTER 14

DISCOVERING THE RIGHT TOOLS
THE STARTER KIT TO HEALTHY RELATIONSHIPS

We are excited to share the following tools we discovered that brought healing to our marriage and family. In fact, many of these tools are still in place to help safeguard our relationship from slipping into old destructive habits and behaviors. Our prayer is that you find this chapter practical in a tangible way.

One of the first steps we took to better our marriage was learning about how God designed us. Having a baseline knowledge of our wiring and how we were created to think and process information, tragedy, and life's influences was enlightening. It gave us a better understanding of why we each responded the way we had in the past. This *awareness* continues to help us be gracious in our acceptance of one another.

AWARENESS – LIMBIC SYSTEM

Dr. Ted and Diane began to educate us on the part of our brain called the limbic system.[13] We learned that our brain is a

---

13. Roberts, D. (2010). *Pure Desire for Women: Eight Pillars to Freedom from love addiction & sexual issues*. Gresham, OR: Pure Desire Ministries International.

very social organism and it is not programmed right out of the box at birth. In fact, it is not until the mid-twenties that one's brain becomes fully developed. The limbic system is developed experientially as a child matures.

Through positive and negative experiences, the limbic system is shaped and becomes part of a person's survival instinct. As one gets older, the limbic system produces chemicals that give good feelings for behaviors that help with survival, as well as chemicals that allow fear and pain to be experienced, which can help protect someone.

As a person gets older, the limbic part of the brain catalogs experiences and therefore shapes what is *safe* and *unsafe* for that individual. When something threatening takes place, the amygdala (within the limbic system), at a *subconscious level* processes that event before the prefrontal cortex (where logic and reasoning come from) can recognize the danger.

It is in those moments that a person can have what is known as a "limbic response." They react without engaging their prefrontal cortex, the part of the brain in the frontal lobe. The prefrontal cortex is where our logic and reasoning come from to help us make sound decisions. Dr. Ted explained how the limbic system is like the boxer, Mike Tyson, and the prefrontal cortex is like the actor, Woody Allen. If in a fight, who do you think will win? *Mike Tyson every time.* The limbic system is powerful, and if not held in check, it could cause a person to make decisions they will regret for the rest of their life.

We learned that every time the limbic system hijacks the brain, a person is making decisions on an emotional level. This is typically a protective reaction to something or someone. They're not thinking *rationally*. They're trying to cope and make the pain or hurt go away as quickly as possible.

CHAPTER 14: DISCOVERING THE RIGHT TOOLS

The limbic system sets up emotional (and behavioral) responses to avoid things that have caused fear and pain, and repeat things that have to do with pleasure and reward. This system is important in understanding coping behaviors. When you do something that takes away stress (to feel normal), the limbic system can associate it with survival, and it becomes part of the craving, pleasure, and reward (do it again) system.

We realized this was taking place at a neurological level for Tiffany, which was part of what drove her to have an affair. For 20 years I caused pain through neglect, verbal abuse, and control—and she finally broke.

In her brokenness, coupled with not having a close relationship with the Lord, Tiffany allowed the enticement of another man to become a way of coping with her pain. Her limbic system associated her immoral behavior with *survival* to feel the love she felt was lacking from me.

It became a craving to fill the void in her heart. And, yes she knew it was wrong at the same time. She often echoed the Apostle Paul's words in Romans 7:19. "For I do not do the good I want to do, but the evil I do not want to do—this I keep on doing." She'd bang her head on the steering wheel, crying out, "Why? Why?" as she was at war with herself.

Dr. Ted and Diane began to coach us regarding the good news that we can learn to deal with our limbic system and the emotional *fight or flight* impulses it gives out from time to time. This powerful part of our brain does *not* give us a pass to say we can't help ourselves and merely cave in to emotion. Instead, through hard work and discipline we can recalibrate and reprogram our knee-jerk emotional responses so that in the future, we don't relapse and cause the very destruction we've experienced.

Tiffany and I work hard, trying to recognize when we have a limbic response to each other or something or someone else. We have given each other permission to point it out to one another lovingly. This causes us to pause and dig deep to not overreact, but rather engage our prefrontal cortex to have a more sound and logical response. It is not easy, but it's doable.

BREATHING EXERCISES

RICK: Breathing exercises became my best friend as a way of coping with emotional hurt and anxiety. The road to recovery was not easy because I experienced triggers often. I remember a phone call I had with Dr. Ted when I was having a moment caused by a trigger. He explained what takes place medically when one stops and does breathing exercises, and went on to share that deep breathing has a direct effect on the nervous system controlling the *fight or flight* in all of us.

Focused breathing relaxes our physical state, which can help us manage stress.[14] Our heart rate and blood pressure can calm down, thus causing relaxation and calmness. He told me that bringing in fresh oxygen through slow deep breaths releases endorphins in the brain, which reduces stress and anxiety. He encouraged me to pause when struggling with anxiety and emotional pain, and do a minimum of three controlled deep breaths.

Doing this sets my body up to receive an endorphin hit that will produce a calming effect and potentially keep me from going limbic. Doing deep breathing has prevented me from saying regretful things to Tiffany, as well as other people. I have learned that it centers my emotions and can keep me from a regrettable action.

---

14. Roberts, T. & Roberts, D. (2012). *Hope for Men: Healing for Broken Trust*. Gresham, OR: Pure Desire Ministries International. 155.

CHAPTER 14: DISCOVERING THE RIGHT TOOLS

THE GOTTMAN

Dr. Ted and Diane realized immediately that we didn't know how to communicate effectively when a regrettable incident took place between us. We argued like immature teenagers who did not listen to each other. Our arguments were always about proving a point.

We spent more energy trying to be heard instead of hearing the other person with the goal of understanding their position. Our conversations were debates done at various volumes. Talking over each other had become commonplace. Our arguments typically ended in disaster, and neither of us felt heard or understood. Our disputes only caused pain and damage to our relationship and caused our kids to feel insecure. We rarely came to an amicable solution.

Dr. Ted and Diane recognized within our first few counseling appointments that we were full of bullet holes from our words. They needed to step in and stop the madness and did so by sharing a valuable tool we still use today.

This tool is what Tiffany and I call "The Gottman." It helps protect us from wreaking more havoc on our already fractured relationship. It is a method we have used with our children and even in the workplace. It is our pleasure to share it with you.

Dr. John and Julie Gottman are therapists who are respected experts in marriage relationships. The two of them have authored best-selling books on the subject. In the Gottman's book, *The 10 Principles for Doing Effective Couples Therapy*, they outline how to effectively communicate when you find yourself at odds with someone, especially your spouse.[15]

---

15. Schwartz Gottman, J. & Gottman, J. (2015). *10 Principles for Doing Effective Couples Therapy*. New York, NY: W. W. Norton & Company.

Tiffany and I have utilized this technique, and it has revolutionized the way we communicate with one another when an offense has taken place. We highly recommend it for everyone, especially married couples.

When we find ourselves at odds with each other because of a word or action, typically one of us says, "Stop, we need to do 'The Gottman.'" We know what that means. At some point that day or evening, we sit down when both of us are calm, and we walk through a *communication process*. The technique that Dr. Julie Gottman came up with helps us express how we're feeling, while at the same time, forces us to *listen* for a better understanding of where the other is coming from. Here is a summary of what Tiffany and I have come to know as "Doing the Gottman."

STEP 1: We take turns sharing what emotions we felt when the offense took place (anger, hurt, being overwhelmed or not being listened to). We make statements like: "During our disagreement, I felt _____." We do not get into the *why* we were feeling the way we did.

STEP 2a: We take turns sharing our perspective—our reality of what happened. This is done in a non-accusatory conversing manner. We avoid statements like, "You did this," or "Because you said _____..."

STEP 2b: After listening to each other, we summarize what we heard the other person say while validating part of or as much of their experience or feelings as possible. Example: "I can see how _____ made you feel the way it did." Or, "It makes sense why you felt _____; I see that."

CHAPTER 14: DISCOVERING THE RIGHT TOOLS

Note: Being willing to see the other's point of view and relate to how the incident made them feel does not necessarily mean you agree with them. You can still *disagree* and *relate* to one's emotion based on their perspective (their reality).

The goal for step 2 is for Tiffany and me to feel heard and understood. If one of us does not, we circle back around the other person's perspective for clarity. We restate our reality again or differently. Once we feel heard and understood, then we move to Step 3.

STEP 3: We try to identify and share a trigger(s) we may have had that fueled an emotional response. Emotional responses can take a simple disagreement and progress it into a full-fledged argument. Therefore, we try to pinpoint a childhood experience we may have felt we were reliving in the moment, or recognize the trigger was caused by an accusatory remark or put-down.

Again, the goal here is to gain a better understanding of what led to the offense. Recognizing and validating one's trigger(s) helps to avoid recommitting the unfortunate occurrence.

STEP 4: We intentionally take responsibility for the conduct that escalated the battle between us. We share if there were other factors involved that played a part in how we behaved. Not to excuse poor behavior, but sometimes life's pressures can set us up for miscommunication. Owning what's going on internally is the responsible thing to do.

STEP 5: We come up with a game plan that will help safeguard us from repeating the issue at hand. Calmly, we each share at least one thing we could personally do next time to help avoid the blow-up, as well as ask the other person to do something different, which could help keep things from escalating. Coming to an agreeable solution will set you up for healthier communication that could protect you from future conflict.

THE FASTER SCALE

We were introduced to something called "The FASTER Scale."[16] The FASTER Scale, explained by Michael Dye in his book, *The Genesis Process*, is a process by which people relapse, potentially leading them back into self-destructive behavior (*of any kind*). Dr. Ted and Diane walked us through the emotional steps we experienced and how to identify when we are *sliding down* The FASTER Scale.

We now know that if we reach the bottom of the scale, we run the risk of repeating unhealthy behaviors that can be potentially destructive to our relationship. What we are about to share is something anyone can learn and apply in every facet of their life, not just within their marriage and other relationships.

PART ONE
// Circle the behaviors on the FASTER Scale that you identify with in each section.

RESTORATION: (Accepting life on God's terms, with trust, grace, mercy, vulnerability and gratitude.) No current secrets; working to resolve problems; identifying fears/feelings; keeping commitments to meetings, prayer, family, church, people, goals,

---

16. Dye. M. (2012). *The Genesis Process: For Change Groups, Book 1 and 2, Individual Workbook* (4th ed.). Ventura, CA: Michael Dye. 233.

CHAPTER 14: DISCOVERING THE RIGHT TOOLS

and self; being open and honest, making eye contact; increasing in relationships with God and others; true accountability.

FORGETTING PRIORITIES: (Start believing the present circumstances and moving away from trusting God. Denial; flight; a change in what's important; how you spend your time, energy, and thoughts.) Secrets; less time/energy for God, meetings, church; avoiding support and accountability people; superficial conversations; sarcasm; isolating; changes in goals; obsessed with relationships; breaking promises & commitments; neglecting family; preoccupation with material things, TV, computers, entertainment; procrastination; lying; overconfidence; bored; hiding money; image management; seeking to control situations and other people.

Forgetting priorities will lead to the inclusion of:

ANXIETY: (A growing background noise of undefined fear; getting energy from emotions.) Worry, using profanity, being fearful; being resentful; replaying old, negative thoughts; perfectionism; judging other's motives; making goals and lists that you can't complete; mind reading; fantasy, codependent, rescuing; sleep problems, trouble concentrating, seeking/creating drama; gossip; using over-the-counter medication for pain, sleep or weight control; flirting.

Anxiety then leads to the inclusion of:

SPEEDING UP: (Trying to outrun the anxiety which is usually the first sign of depression.) Super busy and always in a hurry (finding good reason to justify the work); workaholic;

can't relax; avoiding slowing down; feeling driven; can't turn off thoughts; skipping meals; binge eating (usually at night); overspending; can't identify own feelings/needs; repetitive negative thoughts; irritable; dramatic mood swings; too much caffeine; over exercising; nervousness; difficulty being alone and/or with people; difficulty listening to others; making excuses for having to "do it all."

Speeding Up then leads to the inclusion of:

TICKED OFF: (Getting adrenaline high on anger and aggression.) Procrastination causing crisis in money, work, and relationships; increased sarcasm; black and white (all or nothing) thinking; feeling alone; nobody understands; overreacting, road rage; constant resentments; pushing others away; increasing isolation; blaming; arguing; irrational thinking; can't take criticism; defensive; people avoiding you; needing to be right; digestive problems; headaches; obsessive (stuck) thoughts; can't forgive; feeling superior; using intimidation.

Ticked Off then leads to the inclusion of:

EXHAUSTED: (Loss of physical and emotional energy; coming off the adrenaline high, and the onset of depression.) Depressed; panicked; confused; hopelessness; sleeping too much or too little; can't cope; overwhelmed; crying for "no reason"; can't think; forgetful; pessimistic; helpless; tired; numb; wanting to run; constant cravings for old coping behaviors; thinking of using sex, drugs, or alcohol; seeking old unhealthy people & places; really isolating; people angry with you; self abuse; suicidal thoughts; spontaneous crying; no goals; survival mode; not returning phone calls; missing work; irritability; no appetite.

CHAPTER 14: DISCOVERING THE RIGHT TOOLS

Exhausted then leads to the inclusion of:

RELAPSE: (Returning to the place you swore you would never go again. Coping with life on your terms. You sitting in the driver's seat instead of God.) Giving up and giving in; out of control; lost in your addiction; lying to yourself and others; feeling you just can't manage without your coping behaviors, at least for now. The result is the reinforcement of shame, guilt and condemnation; and feelings of abandonment and being alone.

PART TWO

// Identify the most powerful behavior in each section.

// Answer the following three questions:

1. How does it affect me? How do I feel in the moment?
2. How does it affect the important people in my life?
3. Why do I do this? What is the benefit for me?

DOUBLE BIND

Before counseling, we were unaware of the level of stress someone could feel when he or she is caught in a "double bind."[17] A double bind is when you're stuck between a rock and a hard spot—there is *no easy* answer. A double bind can make a person feel that no matter what decision they make, it is going to be painful. "I'm damned if I do; damned if I don't."

It's when we're caught in these situations that stress and anxiety, often driven by fear, cause someone to start sliding down The FASTER Scale and subject them to relapse.

---

17. Ibid. 57.

We had to learn—and are still learning—how to deal with double binds and navigate our way out of them, which is never easy! To successfully steer your way through such predicaments, it will require a commitment not to shy away from tough decisions and confrontation.

When we find ourselves stuck in these lose/lose situations, a myriad of emotions can flood in—anger, frustration, hopelessness, depression, anxiety, and fear. Typically people tend to numb out by coping in unhealthy ways. We found out that the best way to cope with the double bind is to:

- Identify that we're in a double bind.
- Identify the fear, concern, pain, or discomfort the double bind is causing.
- Seek to understand the origin of why such feelings are present in hopes of bringing personal healing in our lives. This could potentially free us up emotionally the next time this exact double bind occurs.
- Commit to not shying away, but instead facing our fear or concern and do the hard work.
- Chart out our scenario in the Double Bind Worksheet and what would happen if we made certain decisions.

On the next page is a chart that can help walk you through the decision-making process when faced with a double bind. Once filled out, the tough work of carrying it out begins. In the end, you'll be stronger for it and *victorious*, because you made your way through it!

CHAPTER 14: DISCOVERING THE RIGHT TOOLS

DOUBLE BIND WORKSHEET[18]

INSTRUCTIONS: Write out a current problem or situation—involving addictions, fear, control, anxiety, denial, or procrastination. Examine the consequences and risks of both choices. *Example*: If I trust people, I'm vulnerable to being hurt—If I don't trust people, I won't develop relationships. Then apply the formula: If I do what's right, God will bless it, and the right thing to do is usually the hard thing to do.

Next, with accountability and support, make a concrete plan for carrying out your choice. We have examples in the chart below.

Choices	**Problem/Situation:** Control
	If I Do Change (giving up the problem): Healthier relationship with Tiffany
	If I Don't Change (avoiding the problem): Push Tiffany away
Apply	**The Right Thing is the Hard Thing:** My way is not the only way. Discipline. Willing to listen when Tiffany says she's feeling I'm being controlling; step back and assess.
Plan	**What, When, Who, Where, How:** Work on giving Tiffany more of a say. Do not jump in and voice my thoughts right away. Give her a time to speak. Be conscious of this in all settings, one-on-one or in public.

---

18. Ibid. 270.

To make this tool useful, invite a trusted friend to help you identify the consequences of "if I do" and "if I don't." Through probing questions by a friend, not only could they help you see the results of your DO-action or DON'T-action, they may be able to help you see the belief system that drives what's causing the double bind inside of you.

ACCOUNTABILITY

We had to create accountability for one another. Without it, we would go crazy, always wondering how the other one was doing in our journey toward recovery and reconciliation. Holding each other accountable to regain trust was necessary, but it also fostered trustworthiness within our entire family.

For us, accountability was not an attempt to control each other. It was a tool each of us wanted to use to re-establish confidence in our relationship. With a heart of transparency, we voluntarily offered to be held accountable to rebuild faith in each other. This was refreshing since it helped rebuild the bridge of trust that had been destroyed.

If you're in a relationship where you have to work on rebuilding trust, ask your partner to hold you accountable in the areas where trust was broken. It will kick-start the renewal process in your relationship. Healthy accountability gives people checks and balances: it promotes growth and maturity; it provides a level of discipline, and much-needed support to stay on track. We needed to do this for the sake of our marriage and family.

CHAPTER 14: DISCOVERING THE RIGHT TOOLS

// Here are some of the accountability measures we put in place:

FOR TIFFANY (*HER PERSPECTIVE*)

- Have and maintain an active relationship with the Lord.
- Be present and building relationships in our church.
- Be willing to be a part of a small group (if possible).
- Commit to counseling with Rick with Dr. Ted and Diane at Pure Desire Ministries.
- Commit to doing recovery work on a daily basis.
- Commit to being part of an accountability group.
- Submit to a polygraph test and be willing to take a second one if ever asked.
- Turn off all social media for a season.
- Rick has all passwords to social media accounts, email account, iPad, cell phone, etc.
- Allow our children to have my password on my cell phone and iPad.
- Block certain people (social media, email, and phone).
- Rick can receive my texts and emails on his phone.
- Do not keep my phone with me at all times (be willing to let it lay around the house).
- Rick can ask questions anytime if he wanted to check in or if he felt suspicious about something.
- No drinking.

- Actively work on controlling my anger. Work on calming down before going limbic.
- Be willing to work through the Gottman exercise.

FOR RICK (HIS PERSPECTIVE)

- Have and maintain an active relationship with the Lord.
- Work on not treating Tiffany as I would treat my sister (e.g., teasing her).
- Quit trying to control arguments by not giving space.
- Put Tiffany and the kids first.
- Be present when at home.
- Be more proactive in fixing things around the house.
- Deal with tendency to control.
- Do recovery work on a daily basis.
- Be willing to work through the Gottman exercise.

In *The Message*, Paul's words in Colossians 3:16 translate this way: "Instruct and direct one another using good common sense." We knew we needed others, along with each other, to help us maintain *good common sense* for the sake of our relationship and our kids. We invited other people to hold us accountable to positive behaviors.

When dealing with triggers, sliding down the FASTER Scale, and always feeling like we're encountering double binds, we needed a support system to come alongside us. We coached each other, but we heavily relied on certain friends who helped hold us true to our agreed-upon accountability lists. By staying

CHAPTER 14: DISCOVERING THE RIGHT TOOLS

faithful to the lists above, reconciliation, trust, hope, and joy started to become more and more present in our relationship and in our family.

Having the right tools for the right job can make all the difference in the world. If not for the newfound awareness we received about our wiring and how the brain works, the benefits of breathing exercises, the slippery slope of the Faster Scale, the Gottman communication tool, the Double Bind Worksheet, and accountability partners, we are convinced our probability of a successful recovery would have been very low. We encourage you to apply, at a minimum, these tools and search for other great resources.

BIBLIOGRAPHY

Chapman, G. (1995). *The Five Love Languages: How to Express Heartfelt Commitment to Your Mate*. Chicago, IL: Northfield Publishing.

Dye, M. (2012), *The Genesis Process: For Change Groups, Book 1 and 2, Individual Workbook* (4th ed.). Ventura, CA: Michael Dye.

Farrell, B. & Farrell, P. (2008). *The 10 Best Decisions a Couple Can Make: Bring Out the Best in Your Relationship*. Eugene, OR: Harvest House Publishers.

Parrott, L. & Parrott, L. (2006). *Saving Your Marriage Before It Starts: Seven Questions to Ask Before—and After—You Marry*. Grand Rapids, MI: Zondervan.

Roberts, T. & Roberts, D. (2012), *Hope for Men: Healing for Broken Trust*. Gresham, OR: Pure Desire Ministries International.

Schwartz Gottman, J. & Gottman, J. (2015). *10 Principles for Doing Effective Couples Therapy*. New York, NY: W. W. Norton & Company.

Bible.org (n.d.) *Marks of Maturity: Biblical Characters of a Christian Leader*. Mark #16: Accountability. Retrieved from https://bible.org/seriespage/mark-16-accountability.

UNRAVELED

MANAGING LOVE, SEX, AND RELATIONSHIPS

We all want to experience genuine relationship —to feel loved and accepted for who we are. We give and give in relationship only to be left feeling disappointed and alone. Our negative sexual experiences and mistakes from our past hold us hostage, keeping us stuck in unhealthy relationship patterns. Is there any hope?

Through the use of personal stories, strategic tools and exercises, and weekly self-care lessons, *Unraveled* will become our guide. We will discover the core of our distorted beliefs, address the shame that drives our behaviors, and write a new ending to our story, crafted with hope and purpose.

GET YOUR KIT AT **PUREDESIRE.ORG/UNRAVELED**